Acceptance & Obedience
The Life Story of Joseph by the Grace of God

WENDY DAVIE DIP. C. S.

WESTBOW
PRESS®
A DIVISION OF THOMAS NELSON
& ZONDERVAN

WestBow Press books may be ordered through booksellers or by contacting:

WestBow Press
A Division of Thomas Nelson & Zondervan
1663 Liberty Drive
Bloomington, IN 47403
www.westbowpress.com
1 (866) 928-1240

ISBN: 978-1-9736-3626-7 (sc)
ISBN: 978-1-9736-3625-0 (e)

Print information available on the last page.

WestBow Press rev. date: 8/20/2018

PREFACE

For many years, my husband and I travelled throughout the East Coast of Australia from Cairns to Adelaide. We visited many with the intention of encouraging them, either into the faith or in the faith. What a privilege it had been and one we had no real intention of bringing to a halt; however, in 1997 we experienced a serious car accident and our vehicle was destroyed. This brought about a forced change in our lives and the need for us to re-assess our future. There were to be a few more trips, which would involve some extremely difficult times. Only the Lord and those involved would know just how difficult and frightening they were. Therefore, 1998 was a year when we both had a great need to be renewed and strengthened. It was one of grief and a definite need to relinquish evils done to us; thus, learning the ability to forgive. The birth of this study, then, began in the midst of trials, all far more difficult than I felt I could bear. It was sent from the Lord to one of His servants, showing her that as she trusted and obeyed, His strength would see her through. Therefore, I truly add "by the Grace of God." My name is attached, but only as His servant. Since then, many of those who have completed the study have each one voiced my thoughts – "God has blessed me through doing it!" I give Him all the thanks and glory for the exceeding and wonderful riches of His Word and for the leading of His Holy Spirit.

The study has been designed to encourage a daily devotion. If homework is left until the day of your group Bible Study, you may find it will take much longer than six weeks. As well as this, you may find too much reading for one sitting and be left with a less than satisfying study. Feel free to divide the weekly lessons into two if this suits the group better.

1

Wendy Davie Dip. C. S.

You will find that if you do your homework your group study will be enhanced. I encourage you individually to find a suitable time to set aside each day and I know the Lord will bless you abundantly.

May God continue to bless you all
Yours in Christ Jesus,

Wendy

APRECIATION

I wish to extend my appreciation to those who have trialled this study and have willingly given their time and wisdom. Thanks also go to my husband Ewan. Thanks to Don & Helen Stormer, (Retired Principal and his wife of Emmaus Bible College, Epping NSW, Australia), for their faithfulness in the editing of this material; Vera Thomas, a dear friend who proof read the original writing; Margaret Lepke, who is far more knowledgeable with computers than I could ever be and to all others, far too many to mention, who have assisted me in many and varied ways.

DEDICATION

I praise God for His Word, wisdom, discernment and delight: for it was from Him and through His precious Holy Spirit, that this work came into being.

I also wish to dedicate it to my darling husband of nearly 41 years. He was my bosom buddy as "Anne of Green Gables" referred to. It was a delight to treat him like a king, for he always treated me as his queen.

INTRODUCTION

Some years ago, there was a program on TV called "Talking Heads;" it was simply life experiences told personally. Each person only had his or her head in camera frame, but the stories and one in particular, were so heart rending that neither my husband nor I have ever forgotten them. In this Bible Study introduction, I give five short stories involving husbands and their wives, and others, each connected in a small way. We may be tempted to think these stories a little far-fetched, but unfortunately, they are not. They have in fact, each been written from snippets of statements made to us as we have endeavoured to come alongside others.

My "Talking Heads"
(Names and characters used do not intentionally relate to any individual.)

Jenny: I'm sick to death of this family: one day I might just walk out. It's not that I don't love my husband or children – it's just that I'm tired of hassles, always having to be doing for others. I feel as if I've had to give up all my desires in order to slave after others. It just doesn't seem fair. As well as that Bob is always at work. The hours he puts in elsewhere, I can't help but think he must like spending time away from me. He never tells me he loves me anymore. It's as if once we were married he stopped all romantic notions. Life just seems so busy and yet so lifeless. I'm always tired, and really couldn't care less about doing my housework. I don't know what to do, and these kids don't help. I'm always picking up after them. It probably would do them good to suddenly discover I'm gone!

Wendy Davie Dip. C. S.

Bob: There's something wrong with Jenny; I know there is, but I'm dashed if I can work out what is wrong. I know she isn't happy; boy does she let us all know that! She is always angry and snapping at both the children and myself. Nothing seems to satisfy her anymore, I've tried everything I know to make her happy. In the end I just keep working and keep out of the way. When we were having pre-marital counselling, the minister told me never to forget to cuddle her and tell her I love her. However, she is not the same person that I married and it's a bit hard to love someone when they are angry. Sometimes I wonder if the marriage will work and I worry that if it doesn't and she gets the kids; that she will just continue to be angry with them all the time and I don't think that's the way things should be. I know I am away a lot and when I am home – well I just want to sit back and relax with a cold beer and watch the TV: now you tell me, is there anything wrong with that? Once I asked her what was wrong and she said, "nothing" in an obviously false manner. Ugh! What's a man to do anyway? I just don't understand women, a man works hard to bring in the money and there are no thanks, only complaints that you are away too much. They want children and then when they have them – they constantly yell at them. They want a house with nice things, good clothes and plenty of food and then complain about the bills. I tell you I'm ready to walk out, but really don't want to. The old Jenny I married was such fun and good company. It was no trouble at all showing her I loved her, but now if I try – well you know, it's the "no, I've got a headache!" or "I'm too tired." Blessed if I know what to do!

Rose: Jenny thinks she's hard up. I wish my Jack were away more often. At least then I wouldn't get nagged at quite so much. No matter what goes wrong it's my fault. I've even seen him do something stupid and when I told him, before I knew what had happened it was all turned around and once again I was to blame. He shows me no respect and he has taught the children to treat me the same way. Even when I correct them, if he is around, he brushes it off and makes me feel so small. Sometimes I wish he would hit me; anything would seem better than this verbal abuse. Ah well! What are women for anyway, I guess? I just wish I could trust him with my heart and my emotions; in fact, I wish I could tell him how I feel and know he would hear and respect me.

Jack: Why, why did I marry Rose? She is so insipid, always seems frightened and weak. She forgets to do things I ask her to do and then she asks me not to yell at her. Look I was taught that the man was the head of the house and when I try to be that, it never works out. Her dad had the hide to pull me aside one day and give me a book on anger! A book on anger, I tell you: as if it was my problem! What a hide, and in fact what has it got to do with him, interfering with our married life. She corrects me on some silly little things and then wonders why I snap. Well I am just made that way and I can't change, besides why doesn't she just go and fix the problem. – If she loves me like she says she does that is! I always thought a woman's place was in the home and doing housework, but no she had to go out to work and now is always rushing around at home, and still forgetting to do what I asked her. What's the good of missing buttons, you tell me, it may as well be a shed rag. What's the good of a phone when she can't even pick it up to ring the people I ask her to ring. I tell you I'm fed up and so are the children; why they even go off the handle at her as well. One would think she would realize and change her ways.

Anne: I know both Jenny and Rose have their problems, but I just don't have the time to spend with them. I'm always on the run. By the time I run the children to and fro, go to work, do the housework, go to Bible Study and other odds and ends, time always seems to run out. Besides it's so hard to sit and listen to their gripes, especially when they never seem to want to change. If only they'd open their hearts to the Lord, maybe things wouldn't seem so bad. Oh dear…look at all that ironing. One of these days I might catch up. I guess I should pray for them. Maybe if we asked them over for a meal…the trouble is it costs enough to feed our own family, let alone others.

Keith: Keith sat and listened to Anne and what she had been saying about both Jenny and Rose. "Hmm," he said, "I know exactly what you mean." "I certainly don't have time either, besides work and the extra meetings I have to go to." He sat and thought for a while… "I wonder should I be on all these board meetings, it's not just the time, the fact is that I am always running into others with problems myself and they too don't seem to want to change. What disturbs me most is that they all claim to be Christians." "Anne," he said, "people will only change when they want to, sometimes they need to go pretty low, and you are right, we are both overworked and underpaid," he added with a smile. "Besides our financial situation is always running close to the line, so much so, that I find it hard to even have enough to tithe as I believe we probably should do. It does cost a lot to feed a whole family. Maybe we could ask others to pray for your friends – I mean, we will try to pray too, but if others are aware they might help in this way. In the meantime, whenever we see them, don't let it weigh you down, we will just smile and pretend to listen if we have too."

Grandma: Here I sit again in my old rocking chair. Oh dear, oh dear, Lord please help me? Oh dear…my poor Johnny…my poor Johnny. Days come and go: when my darling was alive we did everything together, even sit and rock. Now he's gone, everything's gone. The children are always busy. They say they don't mind spending time with me, but I watch them and I know they are always pushed for time. So, I try not to bother them; and a bother I know I am. Oh dear, I feel just like a clock winding down, no use to myself or to anyone else. I think if I were to fall over and hurt myself…well! They gave me this Vital Call you know, and said if ever I needed help - to press the button, but…what's the use of this life anyway? Dear, dear Johnny how I miss you. Oh Lord! If I fell…I wouldn't care you know. I could just wait there till You took me home too. There, I've taken the Vital Call off and then no one will know any difference. Oh dear, dear, dear Johnny, I hope I can fall.

Grandad: Sadly, he sits outside in the sun; it seems so hard to keep warm these days. When his wife died, he moved to be closer to the children, feeling it a pressure that he should commit himself to do so. However now in a totally new area, with no friends he was finding life just too hard. The companionship of his darling Ruth was a memory he tried desperately to hold on to, but even that seemed to be fading. The family were all reasonably close, but hardly contacted him. Yes, they are busy with work and such, and he remembered what it was like when he and Ruth were bringing up their family, but somehow things seemed to be so different these days. His thoughts wandered over the things that brought sadness to his heart. The children thought he should hand his licence in, but he still felt capable and would be totally trapped if he did. They had no daughters of their own and as lovely as their daughters-in-law were, they did not have the desire to care for him, as his own daughters might have done. Then of course being a man, he knew his sons were just like him and needed their wives to remind them to ring Dad. Shopping was so hard to do, especially with the aches and pains he now suffered. "Lord", he prayed, "We can be surrounded by people and yet be so terribly lonely, please help me to trust you to take me home at the right time?" His dog cuddled up to his bad leg; in spite of the pain it caused, he reached down and patted his pet. "You're my only friend old fella, I guess I best get back to reading this book, what you think?"

Julie: "Here I am – sweet 16 and never been kissed. Even Mum and Dad don't bother now; they just lecture me or yell. No one seems to care about me. The only one who listens is my friend Tom. He wants to kiss me, in fact he wants more than that and I've often been tempted, but he takes drugs and isn't a Christian and besides I'm just too scared. However at least he listens and he says he loves me. I don't know! I don't think I'll ever find someone special: oh, who cares anyhow? What's this love and marriage thing all about anyway? It only seems to be work and more work and no fun. Sometimes I think even adults don't know what love is. I wish they did! I wish I did!"

Tom: "Boy, Julie's a hard nut to crack. I've tried everything I know to open her up to the ways of the world. You know a little bit on the side, but she won't even let me kiss her. Her parents are Christians and she says she is too. Apparently, her dad advised her not to even let anyone kiss her until she knew God had led him or her together. I don't know anything about God, seems to me that if there is a God, he is there just to take all the fun out of life. I know she wants to rebel against them, but it seems she is just too frightened. I told her I love her, well a little white lie won't hurt. She is craving for love and so am I, but all she talks about is marriage – can't see how getting married says someone is in love. What is love anyway? If it feels good just do it - that's what I think!! If she doesn't crack soon I'll go and find someone who will.

We are told in 1Timothy 4:7b to *"exercise yourselves rather unto godliness."* [1]As I thought upon this verse, the one main exercise kept coming to mind. It seemed, in fact, to be as important as the simple exercise of walking – a very basic exercise that should be done automatically – each day by each one of us: it is **acceptance.** When we practice this exercise, it permeates our lives, it brings peace and tranquillity, and when it is not practiced, we are faced with troubles and strife. Each of the above stories have, in fact, showed a great lack of acceptance, and the sorrows faced by each are being completely wasted because of this lack. Unfortunately, people like these are in the majority for all too often the stories may differ, but our feelings are the same. The exercise that should accompany acceptance is **obedience.** For as faith without works is dead, so acceptance without obedience is dead.

How then can we exercise ourselves unto godliness by acceptance and obedience? There are a number of ways and we shall endeavour to discover them as we travel together through the story of Joseph and his brothers.

As you begin each week's lesson, ask God to reveal to you if there are any ways you have failed to accept and obey in your life.

In 1Corinthians 10:11 we read, "**Now all these things happened unto them for examples and they are written for our admonition, upon whom the ends of the ages are come.**"[2] Therefore, we can consider these headings right throughout our study.

- Acceptance of God's holiness and His right to have authority over us.
- Acceptance of the fact that He has had control over our upbringing, our heartaches and sorrows; our joys and delights.
- Acceptance of our sinfulness and our desperate need for salvation through Christ Jesus.

- Acceptance of being born as a man or a woman and the roles in life this brings.
- Acceptance of our spouses and their roles in life.
- Acceptance of the situations we find ourselves in, be they good or bad.

May God bless you as you begin, and travel through these studies; may He grant you the ability to be honest with yourself and especially with Him, and may you have the courage to **accept** any changes needed and then to **obey** completely in all things.

People in the Study

Abraham: His name means "father of a multitude"[3] He was the son of Terah and founder of the Hebrew nation. His family had originally settled in Ur of Chaldees and it appears that they were idol worshippers. He married his half-sister Sarai. His son Isaac was the second of eight, the most prominent three being – Ishmael, Isaac and Midian. Originally his name was Abram until we read of his meeting with God in Genesis 17: he was ninety-nine years old at the time.[4] Then God said to him, *"I am the Almighty God; walk before me, and be thou perfect."*[5] He was a godly man and proved an intercessor on behalf of Lot and his family.

Isaac: His name means "he laughs."[6] He was the only son of Abraham and Sarah. He was probably born at Beer-sheba when Abraham was one hundred years old and Sarah ninety. He would have remembered going through the terrifying experience of his father preparing to offer him as a sacrifice to Almighty God.[7] "A young lad" has a flexible meaning of "servant or young man." [8]Here, it possibly means he was in his twenties or at least in his late teens, but possibly even twenty-five to thirty when this occurred.[9] His mother died when Isaac was thirty-seven. [10]In Genesis 26 we find *"the LORD appeared unto him"* also, and confirmed the precious promises He had previously given to Abraham.[11]

Jacob: His name means "supplanter."[12] He was the younger twin son of Isaac and Rebekah. He secured the birth right by deception, received the blessing and fled to Haran in fear for his life. [13]His parents sent him there in order that he might find a wife from their extended family. He spent many years there and was deceived by his uncle/father-in-law. When he left, without permission, it was with his two wives Leah and Rachel, their two handmaids and all their children.[14]

There were six sons of Jacob and Leah:

Reuben: His name means, "see, a son." [15]He lost his family's respect because of incest with Bilhah. [16]This caused him the loss of his birthright as well. His father described him in Genesis 49 as *"excellent in power, but as unstable as water."*[17]

Simeon: His name means, "hearing."[18] He was a strong zealot type, and he and Levi joined forces to kill the men of Shechem because of the rape of their sister Dinah. Their father was most upset over this and showed his displeasure by calling them *"instruments of cruelty"* – he says they were *"self-willed."*[19] The birthright was passed over them because of this.

Levi: His name means, "joined or attached"[20] and with the above history one need not be surprised. This was the family God later chose for the priesthood.

Judah: His name means, "praise." [21]He was a man of words and had the ability to intercede for others. His father says *"he had the ability to place his hand on his enemies' neck and was the son of a lion's whelp."* [22]This indicates he had discernment as to the best route, and to proceed with caution. Years later our Lord was a descendent of this family.

Issachar: His name means "hire."[23] His life proved his father's prophecy: he was a strong worker and willingly hired himself out or became a servant.[24]

Zebulun: His name means, "dwelling,"[25] he dwelt by the sea.

There were two sons of Jacob and Bilhah. Bilhah was Rachel's maid.

Dan: His name means, "judging."[26] He would judge his people and prove himself *"deceitful as an adder."*[27]

Naphtali: His name means, "wrestling." [28]His father says, *"he was a hind let loose and gave beautiful words."* [29]Maybe he was a man with a lovely singing voice who was always happy.

The next two were the sons of Jacob and Zilpah.

Gad: His name means, "a troop comes" or "good fortune." [30]He would be overcome, but eventually would prove himself an overcomer.[31]

Asher: His name means, "happy." [32]He seems to have been well off and enjoyed the riches and niceties of life.

There were two sons of Jacob and Rachel.

Joseph: His name means, "adding." [33]Because he was the first-born of Jacob's favoured wife Rachel, he tended to spoil Joseph. He was a wise son and showed leadership qualities very early in life. Placing him in the position of "feeding the flock," actually indicates he was shepherding and thus in charge, even though his older brothers were with him. The coat of many colours" was also a symbol of his authority over others, and showed his favoured position among the family. The terms "a son of his old age," or "a wise son," indicate he was a trusted and responsible lad with intelligence beyond his years. He was indeed superior as a leader, but these gifts were not of his making and were not something he should have taken pride in. His brothers resented him, his abilities and his honesty. They also resented the way their father loved Joseph, while he longed for their acceptance and love. This is seen in his self-assertive conversations with them.[34]

Benjamin: His mother originally called him Benoni, meaning *"the son of my sorrow."* His father changed this to Benjamin, meaning, "son *of* *my right hand"* after his mother's death. [35]He was considerably younger than the others were. His father rejoiced at his birth, but sorrowed at the death of his dearly beloved wife.

The family lived in the land of Canaan, near Isaac who lived in Hebron. It appears the older brothers had taken the flocks toward Shechem, which was at least a two-day journey. Possibly they went there, because they did not want to be near the family any more. They certainly did not seem to be in a hurry to return, and we are told that they moved further on to Dothan, which was twenty miles and a day's journey further on. Their enemies lived here too: the Canaanites and Perizzites; therefore, especially after the earlier slaughter of the men of Shechem, Jacob quite understandably became worried for their safety. This family is what we would today call a "dysfunctional family."

Other Points to Note!

Egypt: This was a polytheistic country. This simply means that they believed in many gods. From a biblical perspective, they were immoral in faith and practice. Egypt was an ancient nation, highly civilised and with an extremely well-organized empire.[36]

Potiphar's wife: Potiphar was the captain of Pharaoh's bodyguard. He was probably also in charge of political executions ordered by Pharaoh. An officer or "saris" in Hebrew meant a "eunuch" or "chamberlain." It was customary in ancient pagan countries to require prominent officers in close association to the King to be castrated. This was possibly to ensure their absolute devotion to their duties and also to protect the King from a military coup, which would establish their own dynasty: therefore, it was also done for security of position. If this is the case, his wife may have married Potiphar for financial or political reasons. This gives understanding of her weakness in desiring Joseph, but does not justify it.[37]

STUDY GUIDE

WEEK 1: The dysfunctional family accepting their own sinfulness, yet God's control.

Readings: Genesis 37 – 47:26

Day 1: Gen. 37:1-11; Matt. 7:6; 10:28-32; Prov. 18: 8; and 1Peter 3:15

1. What was there about Joseph that his brothers hated?

2. Is it always wise to tell others how God is dealing with us?

3. How could he have changed the situation in order to bring peace in the family?

4.
   a. Is there ever a time to share our faith with those in our families who don't know the Lord?

15

b. How can this be done in order not to offend?

Day 2: Gen. 37:12-19 and Josh. 24:15

5. How old was Joseph when his father sent him out to look for his brothers?

6. Who touches your heart most in this family, Joseph or his brothers? Explain.

7. When had Joseph's brothers chosen to sin?

8.
   a. What does Rom. 6:19 say about sin?

   b. Comparing James 1:14-15; 4:17; 1John 3:4 and Romans 14:23, explain what you think sin really is?

   c. Who do you think was really behind their sin? Rom 3:23; Isaiah 64:6; Gen. 3:1-13 and Ps. 51:5

Day 3: Gen. 37; re-read verses 20 - 36; John 15:25; Matt. 26:1-5; 14 - 25; and 47 - 56; John 7:3-5 and Psalm 55:12-14.

9. Where was God when all this was happening? Had He lost control?

10. What do you think God may have been teaching Joseph during this horrific time in the pit and being sold eventually into Egypt?

11. Is there any comparison to be made between Joseph and Jesus in these verses?

Day 4: Gen. 39 and Jer. 29:4-7

12. From this chapter, describe the type of man Joseph was, and what his attributes were.

13.
    a. Name some of the things you feel Joseph had to learn to accept.

    b. Did he have a teachable spirit, or did he just accept his situation because he could do nothing else?

    c.   What can be the consequences of the latter attitude?

14.

    a.   What are some of the things we have to learn to accept in our lives?

    b.   Have you accepted them?

Day 5: Gen. 40; Phil. 4:11-13 and 1 Peter 2:20-25

15. Was there bitterness in Joseph's life, or are verses 14 and 15 purely a sign of his acceptance of circumstances, but a natural desire to fight for justice?

16. To whom did Joseph give the glory?

17. What was Paul's attitude to both good and bad situations?

18. What then should be our attitude to unjust suffering?

Day 6: Gen. 41

19. What is the most striking thing about verses 1-13?

20. How did Joseph show praise for God, who He was, and for what He had done in Joseph's life?

21. How did Joseph's faith affect Pharaoh?

22. How had God justified Joseph? In what position did He place him?

Day 7:

23.

    a.   Read Gen. 37: 5-11 and re-read Gen. 41: 33-36. Do you think he had himself in mind as the *"discreet and wise"* man?

    b.   How would he have felt concerning the past thirteen years of sorrow, when he was placed in this position of authority?

Lesson 1 Summary

Our journey through Joseph's life begins with a bad situation. Very quickly we find a bad situation becoming much worse. We could not be blamed for sympathising with Joseph shut up in the pit. He did not know what was to happen to him as he travelled with the Midianites towards a new country and new culture, all far from his father and younger brother. Life certainly did not seem fair to him; it wasn't his fault, surely! All he had wanted was to be accepted by his brothers. As we travel with Joseph it is of utmost importance for each of us to ask, "What is it that you would have me learn LORD?

We see that Joseph's family was dysfunctional (unable to function effectively as a team). This was the case not simply because of the circumstances that they faced from day to day, but also because of their past circumstances. It all began with the fact that Jacob was a deceiver and because he followed his mother's unwise advice. We can read about this in Genesis 27. Then Laban, his father-in-law, deceived him and this led to his marriage to two sisters who were rivals every day of their lives. Their obvious dislike for each other could not help but rub off on their children.

Have we any dislikes for family members? Does our unconscious affinity with one member tend to colour our relationship with others?

The next thing that impresses us is the love that Jacob had for his son. This love was based not on his son's make-up, but rather in his mother: for Jacob loved her more than he did her sister, whom he was deceived into marrying first. In much the same way, we need to always remember that God's love for us is not based on any good thing in us, but rather in the righteousness of His Son and His sacrificial love for us.

Isaiah 64:6 explains

> *"But we are all as an unclean thing and all our righteousnesses are as filthy rags; and we all do fade as a leaf and our iniquities, like the wind, have taken us away."*[38]

In 1John 3:1 we read:

> *"See how great a love the Father has bestowed upon us, that we should be called children of God; and such we are. For this reason, the world did not know us, because it did not know Him."* [39]

And again, in chapter 4:10:

> *"In this is love, not that we loved God, but that He loved us and sent His Son to be the propitiation for our sins."*[40]

Within our families it is important to be aware and accept that we are all individuals and that God deals with us in separate ways. For example, if there are some who have not as yet given their hearts to the LORD, they will not understand our relationship with Him. Non-Christian spouses have been known to become extremely jealous of their Christian partners' first love: "The LORD Jesus."

Joseph's dreams were intended for his own comfort and should not have been used for manipulative purposes. It is of utmost importance too that we do not try to teach others by what the LORD is saying to us, but rather endeavour simply to pray for them and leave them in God's hands. As our children mature and grow, it is important to learn to relinquish them into their Heavenly Father's hands and simply pray for them without ceasing.

Next, we discuss the position of choice. It is important to realize that in each given situation, there is a moment of choice. The brothers' choosing to sin by putting Joseph in the pit had its beginning right back with the unconfessed sins of jealousy, resentment and rage against both their father and Joseph.

In Ephesians 4:22-27 we find:

> *"…that in reference to your former manner of life, you lay aside the old self, which is being corrupted in accordance with the lusts of deceit and that you be renewed in the spirit of your mind and put on the new self, which in the likeness of God has been created in righteousness and holiness of the truth. Therefore, laying aside falsehood, speak truth, each one of you, with his neighbour, for we are members of one another. Be angry, and yet do not sin; do not let the sun go down on your anger, and do not give the devil an opportunity."*[41]

Therefore, as Christians, it is important that we are always quick to confess any sins, for they are more akin to the old nature and we need to be rid of them. Our choices should be the ones our LORD would make; so that we are always able to live to His praise and glory.

All through this week's study we cannot help but see that Almighty God was in control. He is also in control of our lives. This then is the very core of acceptance in our lives. We can meditate on this and understand we are simply His servants. He promises that His love for us is far beyond our understanding, but that He, as our Heavenly Father, will supply all our needs and bless us far beyond what we could ask or think.

In our daily trials, let us remember we are not simply dealing with the visible, but that we are in a spiritual battle.

Ephesians 6:10–18a says:

> *"Finally, be strong in the LORD, and in the strength of His might. Put on the full armour of God, that you may be able to stand firm against the schemes of the devil. For our struggle is not against flesh and blood, but against the rulers, against the powers, against the world forces of this darkness, against the spiritual forces of wickedness in the heavenly places. Therefore, take up the full armour of God, that you may be able to resist in the evil day, and having done everything to stand firm. Stand firm therefore, having girded your loins with truth and having put on the breastplate of righteousness, and having shod your feet with the preparation of the gospel of peace; in addition to all, taking up the shield of faith with which you will be able to extinguish all the flaming missiles of the evil one. And take the helmet of salvation, and the sword of the Spirit, which is the Word of God. With all prayer and petition pray at all times in the Spirit..."*[42]

Joseph, his brothers and his father were not to know what the future would hold, but God did, for He was in control of the future too. This is the case with us also. How blessed we are to have the story of Joseph to help remind us not to waste our sorrows, but to turn them over to the LORD in prayer knowing that we can trust Him fully with our family and all things.

WEEK 2: Accepting that salvation and security comes from God alone.

Readings: Genesis 42, re-read 37

Day 1: Read Summary from Lesson 1

1. What touched you most about last week's lesson?

2. How has this changed your life this week?

Day 2: Gen. 42; Gen. 37:5-11; Matt 18:21-22; Psalm 32:1-5 and Heb. 3:19

3. Was God in control? What did He control? Why?

4. What were the dreams that Joseph remembered?

5.
    a. Suggest some of the thoughts that would run through Joseph's mind during the three days.

    b. Suggest some of the thoughts that would have been in his brother's minds while they were in jail.

Day 3: Gen. 42:1-8; Rom. 1:18-23; 8:5-8; Luke 24: 13-32 and Heb. 3:19

6. Can you think of reasons why Joseph's brothers did not recognize him?

7. Why were the two walking on the road to Emmaus unable to recognize Jesus?

8. What makes us unable to accept God's controlling hand in our circumstances?

9. Does this please God? Cf. Rom.8:8-13

Day 4: Gen. 42:1-28 and Eccl. 3:1-8

10. What comes to mind as you read about the way Joseph speaks to his brothers?

11.
    a. How did the meeting after all these years affect Joseph?

    b.   What do you think caused this grief?

    c.   Is there, then, a time to grieve?

12.

    a.   Three days were involved in their separation. Who else spent three days separated from others and life? Read Jonah 1:17 and Luke 24:19- 24

    b.   Why do you think the three days were important for the following?
          The brothers
          Joseph
          Jonah
          Jesus

Day 5: Gen. 42:21-35; Rom. 2:1; 6:23 and Psalm 32

13. Who was kept as hostage?

14. Whom did the brothers blame for their woes?

15. Whom do you blame when things appear to be going wrong?

16. Does God use our sorrows? Note Psalm 32:8,9.

Day 6: Gen. 42:35-38 and Rom. 8:14-17

17. Whom did Jacob blame?

18. What was he failing to do?

19. As Christians what have we lost and what have we gained?

Day 7: Psalm 32

20. What makes us blessed? Cf. Col.2:14

21. What happens when we don't confess our sin?

Wendy Davie Dip. C. S.

22. To whom should we acknowledge our sin?

23. When should we come near to God in prayer? Cf. 1 Thess.5:17

24. What does David mean by "You are my hiding place"?

Lesson 2 Summary

One night, my husband and I arrived home late and in sheer exhaustion sat in the lounge chairs for a little rest and chat before retiring. We both sat there looking up at the light in the centre of the ceiling. There, to our surprise, was a little ant. We watched as this ant made the circumference of the light surround. After some time of watching its travels, we began counting each circuit. To our amazement, we counted over one hundred full circuits and the ant continued even after this. The LORD spoke to our hearts that night, for it seems that many of us go around in circles in our lives and never find the way of escape. We do this in many different ways. We worry and fret over problems that always seem so big at the time. When our house was full of young people, I discovered a very important fact – although the troubles, which came upon us, appeared so large; if we prayed about them, within minutes they had already begun to change!

This week's lesson is all about problem solving. Joseph and his brothers had serious problems and their gracious loving Almighty God knew their failings, their past sins and the weaknesses of the flesh in each of them. Almighty God loved them in spite of those things that caused them to struggle and react to each other and the circumstances within the family. He loved them so much that He wanted them to be reconciled to each other. In fact, more than this; He wanted the family to become functional and united and He wanted to keep His promises to Abraham, Isaac and Jacob and so become the God of their children.

Nowhere in the Scriptures do we find it said of Joseph that he was a godly or faithful man. Some commentators say he was a type of

Christ. This is possible and certainly we find many things we can compare between them, but it is interesting to note that there is no mention of Joseph ever meeting face to face with God. Abram did and became Abraham. He received great and precious promises and we are told that he was a man of faith. Isaac met God and the promises were renewed. Jacob met God and his name became Israel. We read of Joseph's problems one after another and we read that he and others surrounding him were blessed. Yet still the problems continued. As we study, we cannot help but see that sometimes God brought the problems upon him, while in other cases, God allowed the problems that swept in upon Joseph. It is interesting to realize though, that with each problem Joseph grew closer to the LORD and his faith was evident not only to those he lived with, but also to us today. Joseph had a simple faith; he believed that God is and that He was the giver and the only one who revealed dreams. Although he was married to the daughter of the priest of On, this did not alter his faith in God.

("On" means "abode" or "city of the sun". It was a town in Lower Egypt and is better known under its Greek name of "Heliopolis;" it is called Beth-She'mesh in Jeremiah 43:13.) [43]

This is where he was sent as a slave and this is where he had lived for the previous twenty years. He watched the Egyptians live out their belief system in their entire daily lives; one that involved the worship of many gods, yet he remained faithful to the One true God.

When his brothers arrived to buy grain, Joseph could have chosen to ignore them and not to even communicate with them. Bitterness and grief could have caused him to say in his heart,

"I don't want to have anything more to do with them. Just sell them the grain and send them on their way." However, he did not do so. In our problems, we too, need to make choices and it is in the making of these choices that we are able to escape the treadmill of simply going around in circles, like our ant. Joseph made the choice for God; and so, he decided to test his brothers' love for their father and Benjamin. He wanted to see if there was any remorse over their past sins.

The brothers were acting just like people without any Christian ethics: they were not spiritually minded. The two people on the road to Emmaus were like this also. (Remember we looked at them on Day 3 and Question 7). Unfortunately, this can be the case with us too! Oh yes, we may be Christians, but sometimes we can be so taken up with our worldly life and efforts, that we don't even talk to the LORD unless a problem arises. Paul explained to the Corinthian Church that this was their problem; they too were *"carnal, even babes in Christ."* (1 Cor.3:1)[44]

> He adds in verse 3, *"...for you are still fleshly. For since there is jealousy and strife among you, are you not fleshly, and are you not walking like mere men?"*[45]

In James 1:13-15 we read:

> *"Let no one say when he is tempted, 'I am being tempted by God'; for God cannot be tempted by evil, and He Himself does not tempt anyone. But each one is tempted when he is carried away and enticed by his own lust. Then when lust has conceived, it gives birth to sin; and when sin is accomplished, it brings forth death."*[46]

So then to begin solving our problems, we must first honestly face ourselves before a holy and righteous God and ask, "LORD is this problem due to some sin in my life?" If the answer is yes, we must accept the truth and confess the sin, then start afresh. If we find as Joseph did, that it is a problem God allowed because of another's sin, then accept that too and pray for wisdom and strength in order to overcome in Christ Jesus our LORD.

We need also to pray fervently for the one who has wronged us, in order that bitterness will not be given a foothold upon us.

James 1:2-6 and verse 8 is worth remembering:

> *"Consider it all joy, my brethren, when you encounter various trials, knowing that the testing of your faith produces endurance. And let endurance have its perfect result, that you may be perfect and complete, lacking in nothing. But if any of you lacks wisdom, let him ask of God, who gives to all men generously and without reproach, and it will be given to him. But let him ask in faith without any doubting, for the one who doubts is like the surf of the sea driven and tossed by the wind…being a double-minded man, unstable in all his ways."*[47]

Then again in verse 12:

> *"Blessed is a man who perseveres under trial; for once he has been approved, he will receive the crown of life, which the LORD has promised to those who love Him."*[48]

We discovered this as we studied Psalm 32. It was here also in verse 7 that we found David exclaiming to God, *"You are my hiding place."* The wonderful joy is that no matter what the problem is, we too can truly say the same.

> **"You are my hiding place; You preserve me from trouble; You surround me with songs of deliverance."** [49]

Peace

Amidst the turmoil and heartache of the world;
I have peace.
Like a country river, bubbling along;
I have peace.
As a bird sings out for joy;
I have peace.
The cows in the meadow, the crows in the corn,
A butterfly floats by and
I have peace.
Guns of war shout their news of anguish and pain;
Sorrow breaks my heart, but...
I have peace.
For my Lord shall return as He went before:
Praise God...I have peace.

Thank you, Lord, for being my "Hiding Place."

WEEK 3: Accepting that our walk must be one of faith

Reading: Genesis 43

Day 1: Read Summary notes

1. What touched you most in last week's lesson?

2. How has this affected your daily walk with the LORD?

Day 2: Gen. 43; Prov. 3:5-8 and Gen. 49:8 and 9

3. What was it that brought about Jacob's attitude of acceptance in verse 14?

4.
   a. Did Joseph's brothers have a daily relationship with God?

   b. Which verses indicate this and why? Cf. Gen. 42:37

   c. How can we have a daily relationship with God?

5.

   a.   Who did Joseph continue to give the glory to in his life?

   b.   Had the hard lessons of life then, been wasted?

6.   What is the lesson we can learn from verse 30?

Day 3: Gen. 42:29, 36; 43:11; Acts 9:1-20; 13:9; 22:1-16 and 26:9-18

7.   What is the significance of this name change from Jacob to Israel?
     Cf. Gen.35:10 & 32:28

8.   What sort of man was Saul, prior to his road to Damascus conversion?

9.   What brought about his conversion?

10. What sort of man was he after his conversion?

Wendy Davie Dip. C. S.

Day 4: Hebrews 11

11. What is faith?

12. Why is it necessary?

13. What should we believe about God? Note verse 6.

14. In the examples of the faithful Old Testament saints given here, what were Jacob and Joseph noted for?

15. Does this speak to your heart?

Day 5: Genesis 43:11-15

16. Was Israel showing faith or acceptance here?

17. Give the dictionary meanings of
    a. Faith:

    b. Acceptance:

Day 6: Genesis 43

18. Name the things in this chapter that need to be accepted and by whom?

19. Can you relate to any of these?

Day 7: Gen. 43; Heb. 11:1-3 and Rom. 10:17

20. Name those who were obedient in the Genesis reading and how?

21. What acts of obedience do we find hard?

22. Re-read Hebrews 11: 1-3 and Romans 10: 17

    a. How then do acceptance and faith relate to each other?

    b. Explain what you believe faith to be?

Lesson 3 Summary

During this past week we have entered the lives and homes of Joseph, Jacob and the eleven brothers. We can look back in hindsight and see how God had been dealing with them. We saw how Jacob continued to grieve over the loss of his son Joseph, and found it hard to make the transition from striving to protect his youngest son, to a place of relinquishment, rest and trust in God. We can imagine how Joseph felt as he waited the months it took for his family to return. How many times must he have asked God if he had made the right decision, if he had said the correct thing! Can you see him often going down into the prison watching Simeon secretly and quietly talking to God about the possible future events?

We cannot help but imagine how the brothers felt. They must have seen their father's torment, watched the store of food depleting, missed Simeon, and tormented themselves with the thoughts of guilt, impatience and shame. They could only look at Benjamin and realize that he was their one hope of survival and wonder what his absence would do to their father.

To enable this still dysfunctional family to begin moving forward in their lives, God needed to produce certain changes. Firstly, He needed to bring Jacob to a place where his name change became a life change. He needed to recognize that Almighty God truly is God who brings these promises to pass. He needed to know that God and God alone, had the power over life and death; and that he, Jacob, could not fight against God. He needed to learn to trust Him with his life, the lives of his children and their families. He needed to forgive his sons for their failings and begin to trust them as well.

The next change that was needed was in the hearts of the brothers. Each of them needed to know that God cared for them and that He forgave them for their sinfulness. They also needed to know that God is the Almighty and that He controlled their lives, both in life and death. They needed to humble themselves and begin to be willing to serve God where He placed them, in the roles He placed them and in the family position where He had placed them.

Finally, Joseph needed to show God and himself that he had truly forgiven his brothers. He needed to know that his brothers had changed and that God had forgiven their sin. He also needed to know that God understood his loss and the need to forgive as well as understand the grief of his father and brother Benjamin.

Each of these lives was at a different place in their relationship with God. Some were in the early stages of their walk with God, whilst others appear to be further along the road. As we look at the tapestry of their lives we can see that God alone is in total control. Can we see His guiding hand upon their lives and His patience in waiting while they worked through their thoughts and feelings?

This week we also looked at the place of faith in their lives and in ours.

In Hebrews 4:10 we read:

> *"For he that is entered into his rest, **he also hath ceased from his own works**, as God did from His."* [50]
> **(boldness added for further understanding)**

Earlier in this chapter we find the writer speaking of a special rest that is left for us to enter. He says in verse 6 that some did not enter their rest.

> *"Seeing therefore, it remaineth that some must enter into it, and they to whom it was first preached entered not in because of unbelief."*[51]

Verse 11 adds:

> *"Let us labour, therefore, to enter into that rest, lest any man fall after the same example of unbelief."*[52]

What then is this place of **rest**?

It is a place of abandonment into God's loving care…in everything… always. It is understanding that my striving to do my own works is a place of unbelief.

This then is the place to which God was directing Jacob, Joseph and the eleven brothers. That place of rest, knowing that God is; and that He is working it out.

In 1Chronicles 28:9 we read:

> *"As for you, my son, Solomon,* **know the God of your father,** *and serve Him with a whole heart and a willing mind; for the LORD searches all hearts, and understands every intent of the thoughts. If you seek Him, He will let you find Him, but if you forsake Him, He will reject you forever."*[53]
>
> **(boldness added for further understanding)**

"Strong's Concordance" explains that the word, **"know"** or **"yaw dah"** in Hebrew, simply means, "to ascertain by seeing." It is a belief brought about by personal experience.[54] It is not knowledge gained through being taught by others, or by cunning ways, or by our own intelligence. That is, it is not something we gain by mentally absorbing information in an analytical method, *but rather by experiencing God's love and grace in our personal lives. This can only be done by faith* – it is not practicing emotional experience!

This is what Jacob's family were doing: learning by watching God work in their lives and experiencing His grace, love and forgiveness. Firstly, they faced themselves and then accepted their own wretchedness before a holy and righteous God. They recognized their need for His saving grace; next, they stepped aside and allowed God to direct their lives, by ceasing from their own works. It was only then that they all began to rest in Him in all aspects. Jacob reveals this action in Genesis 43:14

> *"And God Almighty give you mercy before the man, that he may send away your other brother, and Benjamin. If I be bereaved of my children, I am bereaved!"* [55]

This then, is what we must do also. We can know of God, because we have read the Bible, or have been told of Him, His love and His grace. We can know of God, because of our parent's faith - but until we face ourselves, recognize our own wretchedness, His holiness and our need for salvation – all is pointless! We must meet Him, just as Paul did on the road to Damascus. It is here we understand that He changes our lives and forgive us. Until this time we shall never really ***"know the God of our fathers and be able to serve Him with a whole heart and with a willing mind."*** [56]We shall never accept with grace in our hearts ourselves, our rolls as men and women, our families (with all their differences), our attitudes towards work, or whether we are single, married, widowed, with or without children – unless we do! Whatever our lot we need to accept it as God-directed, God-protected and then we must live in obedience, faithfully resting on Him and His work in our lives.

WEEK 4: The family accepted that it was chosen and therefore needed to be set apart for God.

Readings: Genesis 44, 37 and 49

Day 1: Read Summary notes

1. What was the dictionary meaning of acceptance?

2. What blessed you most from last week's study?

3. What changes have you decided to make because of this knowledge?

Day 2: Gen. 37: 20-36; 44:1-7 and 27b-34

4. Why do you think Joseph asked his steward to deceive his brothers?

5. Had they changed?

Day 3: Gen. 44:1-13; 43:23; 1Peter3:1 and Eph. 5:22-33

6. Do you think the steward was privy to the reason why Joseph had asked for this deception?

7. Did he then obey? What could his possible thoughts have been?

8. Do we always understand when we are asked to obey those in authority over us – be they Elders, bosses, parents, husbands or God?

9. Can you do this – that is, be obedient – even if you don't understand?

Day 4: Gen. 44:14-17; Gen. 37:5-11 and Heb. 4:12 and 13

10. What do these verses in Genesis reveal?

11. What do you think Joseph was saying in verse 15?

12. What does the Hebrews reading tell us?

Wendy Davie Dip. C. S.

13. In verse 16, what was Judah acknowledging?

Day 5: Gen. 44:18-34 and 37:20-36

14. Was Judah any better than the others?

15. Whose son, was he? (Gen. 29:32–35)

Day 6: Gen. 44:16-34; Heb. 4:12-16; 10:31; Rom.3:23 and 6:23

16. What was the aim of Judah's speech?

17. Did Benjamin need Judah to intercede? Explain.

18. Do we need an intercessor? Explain.

19. Who does this for us? (Heb. 7:24 and 25)

Day 7: Gen. 49:1-28 (NIV or NASB use may be wise.); Heb. 7:14; Matt. 1:1-3; extra reading Gen. 35:22; Heb. 11:21 and 22 and extra reading Gen. 35:22

20. Reuben is mentioned in Genesis 37:20-36. Write down your thoughts concerning him now that you have read Genesis 49.

21. Simeon was mentioned in Genesis 42:21-24. Why do you think Joseph chose him to remain as hostage?

22. What does Jacob say about Judah?

23. Re-read Genesis 44:33,34; Matthew 26:36-46; Rom. 6:23. What did Jesus do for us?

Lesson 4 Summary

Many years ago, as a young married woman, I struggled from day to day unable to ever achieve life in its fullness. On the outside I probably seemed happy enough. Certainly, I loved my husband and family and was often seen to relax, enjoying a good laugh and chat with neighbours, both over the fence and visiting for coffee. The signs were visible to a discerning heart though, in that I wasn't happy at home or with my own company. Our home did not appear too bad though and like most people with problems, I learned to hide the signs; but God knew that it was a mess, just like my life. One of my heart's felt catch cries was, "but what about me?" Like most women I grew up dreaming of a husband, family and my own home. The strange thing was that I had all this, yet still struggled with depression.

In this week's study, we could not help see that Benjamin too may have felt, "but what about me?" Can you imagine him saying, "No-one asked me how I felt about all this? Yes, I wanted to come to Egypt. After all, before this I'd hardly travelled twenty kilometres from home. Thought it would be a real buzz…but this is a bit over the top. I've always dreamed of travel, but I never wanted to stay away long. Look, I've been framed. I didn't steal anything, let alone his stupid silver cup!"

Remember our first "talking head" on page five? Jenny felt she had to give up all her desires in order to slave for others. She had never planned this; neither had I; and neither did Benjamin. Do you also have these feelings at times? If someone had asked me then, "Well what are your desires, what do you want to do?" I guess it would have been hard to find an answer. Yes, I loved my husband and I loved my children, and our home; but something was wrong: I just felt used! If I filled my life with hobbies or work for example, would that have helped? No! For looking back in hindsight, I realize my problem was one of acceptance. Having any number of my desires fulfilled, would have only served to prevent me from facing up to this basic problem. What did I need to accept? I needed to accept that God had made me a woman, and a mother, with my weaknesses and strengths; (I had wanted it, but on my terms, not God's)

As children we all long for security, self-acceptance and love, if our parents, quite unintentionally at times, fail to lead us to these things through the cross of Christ; we spend the rest of our lives searching for them in other areas of life.

How important then, for us to grasp the big picture, not in Benjamin's life, but in ours; God is in control: He made us. He knows our needs, our spouses, children, our neighbours and our Church families. He works all these needs together into His tapestry of life. To us life will not always seem fair, but we are not God and do not know why one trouble or another might come upon us. We, like Benjamin, may not be guilty of bringing this trouble upon ourselves, but sometimes God needs to take us to a low point in order to help someone else. Without Benjamin as a "tool for service," his brothers could never be freed from their chains of guilt and sin. Without his being a "tool for service," Joseph could never have shown his great love. Without him, the family would never have been united.

Joseph did not take him aside and say, "look Benjamin, always remember that I love you. Just go along with what happens; I believe in you, but I just have to do this, OK?" If he had, Benjamin might not have managed to carry out the acting role he needed to. He could not have understood, because he too did not know of Joseph's great love. Even if he had been partially aware of this love, he could not have grasped it in full. This too, was my trouble, I knew God loved me and I always had a respect for Him and His Son. I had given my heart to Him, but had never learned to trust Him. I rebelled against life, routine, loneliness, housework (ironing, making beds and washing-up especially: rebelling against being told what to do. The difficulty here was that my husband would have said, "but I never told you what to do," and he would have been right. Unfortunately, my heart did the telling and decency spoke loud and clear. I needed to make a full transition from being a citizen of the world to a citizen of heaven, with a purpose and goal in life. I needed to accept my life as "a tool for service" for God in His tapestry of life. Now we are all "tools for service" – some are clean and shiny, ready for use, others are a little stiff, whilst some are nearly useless.

What makes us useless? *The rust and grit that prevents us is rebellion, our unwillingness to accept that God is God and our Creator.* He has the right to make us His special "tools for service" pleasing to Him, just as He desires. He has made us men and women. Many are parents, while others are called to a life of singleness or barrenness, (these are often used by God to minister to others.) We do not need to understand fully why we are like we are, and in most cases, it is far better not to know. Although many would disagree, the roads are similar in hardness.

- o To be a teenager is tough, wanting to be able to be in control and make decisions for ourselves, yet still hungering for our parents to guide us.
- o To be a husband or wife is not easy.
- o To be a parent is quite difficult at times, especially if our children are disabled, sick or become wayward. Parenthood takes great wisdom and the ability to carry many jobs without training.
- o It is not easy to be single, as there is always emptiness in our heart and until we can learn to lean on the LORD for that closeness we desire - life is hard.
- o It is not easy to be without children and many times the craving from this God-given desire is so great, it seems as if our hearts will break: (women especially feel this, as it is part of a healthy yearning for them to carry a child and bless their husband.)
- o It is not easy when we lose our loving spouse.

- o It is not easy either to have gone through divorce and broken marriages
- o Neither is it easy to be old and failing with no kin to come along side us.
- o Nor is it easy either to live lives of ill health: some have daily struggles with life and death.

Benjamin would probably never have left home, if he had known what he would have been accused of. He was not finding life easy either. However, rebellion does not work; it only brings stress and heartache.

What makes us stiff? *It is self-centredness that does this.* We do not accept with joy in our hearts the role of servant hood for God and instead wallow in the misery of self-pity. What faith we have is weakened, we become like grass blown by the wind, for unconsciously we are striving to worship two gods. The Almighty and ourselves!

What makes us clean and shiny? *Confessing our need for Christ in our lives, being fully cleansed by Him and filled with His Holy Spirit.* Willingly accepting His great love, learning to trust Him as our Master and so placing ourselves in His hands to be used wherever, whenever, and however He chooses. This brings great joy and delight to us and opens the door for others to learn of His great love for them.

> *"Behold what manner of love the Father hath bestowed upon us, that we should be called the children of God."* 1John 3:1a[57]

Our LORD showed us a great example of servant hood:

> *"Who, although He existed in the form of God, did not regard equality with God a thing to be grasped, but emptied Himself, taking the form of a bond-servant, and being made in the likeness of men. Being found in appearance as a man, He humbled Himself by becoming obedient to the point of death, even death on the cross."* Phil. 2: 6-8[58]

Yes, He intercedes for us. Let us also endeavour to have the same attitude not just this week but always. Let us delight in being His **"tools for service"** cleansed and ready for use. We too shall be encouraged as He reveals His great love for us.

WEEK 5: Accepting True Healing

Readings: Genesis 45

Day 1: Read Summary notes

1. Was there anything new that you discovered from last week's lesson? Explain.

2. How has this new knowledge helped your Christian life?

Day 2: Gen. 45:1-3; Ex. 20:1-17; Rom. 3:23 and Phil. 2:9-11

3. When Joseph at last revealed himself to his brothers, why couldn't they answer him?

4. What made them so afraid?

5. What was it that they needed?

6.
    a. What does Paul say every man's reaction to Jesus will be?

b.   Does this happen today?

Day 3: Gen. 45:1-8 and Heb. 4:14-16

7.   Joseph said to his brothers, "Come near to me, I pray you." Can we come near to God in a similar way?

8.   Why were they frightened to come near? Cf. Gen.42:21 and 22

9.   Look up the following verses and explain what stops us from coming near to God.

John 3:16–21

Psalm 32:3-5

Psalm 66:18

Isaiah 59:2

2Timothy 3:5

1Timothy 4:7b

10.

    a.   Why was Joseph in Egypt?

    b.   Why are you where you are?

Day 4: Gen. 45:1-8; Rom. 8:28-39 and 11:5

11. What does Romans 8:28 and 29 indicate?

12. How many years of famine were still remaining?

13. How was God showing His mercy and grace to the children of Israel?

14. Is there anything in your life that you find hard to accept at this present time?

Day 5: Gen. 45:1-15; Matt. 26:28; 1John 4:7-10 and John 15:9-11

15. Read Gen. 45:6–15. Describe all that God had done.

16. Can you describe what He has done for you?

17. Look back at question 14 and re-read Romans 8:28-29. What are your thoughts now?

Day 6: Gen. 45:16-20

18.

    a.   What was Pharaoh's reaction to the report of Joseph's family coming?

    b.   Why do you think this was the case?

19. What did Pharaoh tell them to do?

Day 7: Gen. 45:16-28; Phil. 3:13 and 14 and 2Cor. 5:17-21

20. What life changes would this move have brought to Jacob and his family?

21.

    a.   Apart from the fact that they might have starved due to the famine, why else did they determine to go?

    b.   Why should we be obedient to the LORD?

22. Read again the NT references. How should we be obedient to the LORD?

Lesson 5 Summary

> *"See how great a love the Father has bestowed on us, that we would be called children of God, and such we are."* 1John 3:1a[59]

Chapter 45 is filled with God's grace and joy. In spite of their past sins, Joseph's brothers discover the grace that only Joseph could give them, because as well as sinning against God, they had also sinned against Joseph.

We too have sinned against our God. Psalm 51:3 and 4 says:

> *"For I acknowledge my transgressions, and my sin is ever before me. Against thee, thee only, have I sinned, and done this evil in thy sight, that thou mightest be justified when thou speakest, and be clear when thou judgest."*[60]

He, as the Almighty God, has shed His grace upon us, and therefore He is also the only One who can cleanse and forgive.

Many years had passed for the family and during these years they had learned, as many of us do, to bury their sins and failures in the sea of forgetfulness. Yes, on occasions these sins would come to mind, but had they truly dealt with them before a holy and righteous God?

When we first give our hearts fully to the LORD, we can find ourselves in such a euphoric state; all our past sins have certainly gone. We have become new, that is from God's perspective. The trouble is, there are often memories of past sins that sometimes trouble us. Have we laid them at the Saviour's feet? Also, there may be weaknesses of the flesh that easily beset us and can be used by Satan to pull us down and cause us to stumble in our Christian walk. Is it possible that this is what had happened to the ten brothers? Had they tended to say in their hearts, "Ah well - past is past! There is no sense bringing it up now. We won't tell Dad what really happened. We might be kicked out of house and home and he will still grieve. In fact, his grief may be increased. No, we'll just learn from our lesson, sacrifice a beast to cover our sin and determine in our hearts never to fall into that trap again."

The unfortunate part of some 'confessions' is that they can become part of an 'easy religion.' As long as one fulfils the regulations and keeps one's head down, everything seems fine. However, one's conscience can still tick over. This is as true today as it was in the past. The Christian faith is the only one that cleanses the conscience.

In Hebrews 9:1, and 6-10 we are told:

> *"Now even the first covenant had regulations of divine worship and the earthly sanctuary...Now when these things have been thus prepared, the priests are continually entering the outer tabernacle, performing the divine worship, but into the second only the high priest enters, once a year, not without taking blood, which he offers for himself and for the sins of the people committed in ignorance. The Holy Spirit is signifying this, that the way into the holy place has not yet been disclosed, while the outer tabernacle is still standing, which is a symbol for the present time. Accordingly, both gifts and sacrifices are offered which cannot make the worshipper perfect in conscience, since they relate only to food and drink and various washings, regulations for the body imposed until a time of reformation."*[61]

Joseph said to his brothers, *"Come near to me I pray you."* We too are encouraged in the Word of God in Hebrews 10:22 for it says:

> *"Let us draw near with a sincere heart in full assurance of faith, having our hearts sprinkled clean from an evil conscience and our bodies washed with pure water."*[62]

As they drew near to Joseph, his love and tears washed them clean. As we draw near to our LORD we too can discover this.

The wonderful aspect of becoming 'children of God' is that we should no longer be troubled in conscience. Hebrews 9:11-14 continues:

> *"But when Christ appeared as a High Priest of the good things to come, He entered through the greater and more perfect tabernacle, not made with hands, that is to say, not of this creation; and not through the blood of goats and calves, but through His own blood, He entered the holy place once for all, having obtained eternal redemption. For if the blood of goats and bulls and the ashes of a heifer sprinkling those who have been defiled, sanctify for the cleansing of the flesh, how much more will the blood of Christ, who through the Eternal Spirit offered Himself without blemish to God, cleanse your conscience from dead works to serve the living God?"*[63]

It is possible the ten brothers had honestly come before the LORD and confessed their sin. If this were the case, meeting up with Joseph would still have given them an awful shock, for they thought he was dead. Joseph was quick to re-assure them their sin was forgiven; for God had shown him that He had allowed it for His glory.

As we re-read Genesis 45: 3-8, we cannot help seeing Joseph's forgiving, gracious heart. He had come a long way. Yes, he still acknowledged his brothers' sin, for we read of him saying in verse 4b *"whom you sold into Egypt."* This is not done in an unforgiving spirit, but simply to help them see that the Almighty overrules in the lives of His chosen people. He is the God who controls. Does this then mean that God is the author of evil? Did He put it into the hearts of the brothers to treat Joseph in such a dreadful way? God forbid! James 3:13-18 explains:

"Who among you is wise and understanding? Let him show by his good behaviour his deeds in the gentleness of wisdom. But if you have bitter jealousy and selfish ambition in your heart, do not be arrogant and so lie against the truth. This wisdom is not that which comes down from above, but is earthly, natural, demonic. For where jealousy and selfish ambition exist, there is disorder and every evil thing. But the wisdom from above is first pure, then peaceable, gentle, reasonable, full of mercy and good fruits, unwavering, without hypocrisy. And the seed whose fruit is righteousness is sown in peace by those who make peace."[64]

We see that their sin was wrong, but God in grace brought everything about for His glory.

Many books and studies today speak about the 'healing of the memories.' It is important for us to know the difference between the "New Age memories" and conscience of sin. God healed Joseph from the memory of his brothers' sin. He does this for us too, when during our lives we have to face trying or difficult circumstances. Is this what "New Agers' mean? No! They suggest we all have memories of past lives. Bad thoughts and actions are supposed to affect us whilst being carried in the womb. There is no scriptural basis for this concept. What we need is a cleansing of our conscience: accepting Jesus Christ as God's perfect substitute for us can only do this. He is God's Son, who went into the Holy of Holies and offered His own blood as a living sacrifice for us. Being God, who became flesh for us, He is pure and without sin and therefore He is the **only acceptable sacrifice for us.** The cleansing continues as we accept His Word as truth and trust Him when He says in 1John 1:9:

"If we confess our sins, He is faithful and righteous to forgive us our sins and to cleanse us from all unrighteousness."[65]

It is also important to accept that when Satan reminds us of our past faults, we have been made new in Christ Jesus.

> *"Blotting out the handwriting of ordinances that was against us, which was contrary to us, and took it out of the way, nailing it to His cross. And having spoiled principalities and powers, He made a show of them openly, triumphing over them in it."* Col. 2:14-15[66]

We then can say, "Get behind me Satan, for the day I accepted Jesus Christ's sacrifice for me, I was washed clean by His blood and those sins can no longer be held against me."

Note the love God had for Joseph and his brothers. He allowed, because He loved; and He sent, because He wished to preserve them. This He also does for us, but, as noted earlier in this study, we are all "tools for service." It is our responsibility always to be ready for service in righteousness and wherever we are, to continue to praise Him as the Almighty God.

> *"And we know that all things work together for good to them that love God, to them who are the called according to His purpose. For whom He did foreknow, He also did predestine to be conformed to the image of His Son…"* Rom. 8:28-29a [67]

While in this state of acceptance we too, like Paul, can say:

> *Brethren, I do not regard myself as having laid hold of it yet;* **(that is perfection)** *but one thing I do: forgetting what lies behind and reaching forward to what lies ahead, I press on toward the goal for the prize of the upward call of God in Christ Jesus."* Phil 3:13-14[68]
> **(Section in bold and brackets added for clarity.)**

As our memories are cleansed we can rest in His love and grace.

WEEK 6: Learning from Joseph and his family

Day 1: Gen. 45:21-28; Mark 9:14-29 and 16:1-14

1. Note the name change again in verses 25–28. Why was this so?

2. Did the disciples struggle with an "up and down" attitude to belief?

3. What was the father's prayer in Mark 9?

Spend some time in prayer. Deal faithfully before God. If necessary, confess any known sins and begin praising Him for who He is and what He has done for you in Christ Jesus.

> There may be a need for you to glance over your questions and answers from the previous weeks.

Day 2: Gen.1: 1; John 1 and Psalm 139:13-16

4. *"In the beginning God made Heaven and earth."* Meditate on this and give your comments.

5. When do you think it was that Joseph began to recognize God as the Almighty and that He was in total control of Joseph's life, both good and bad?

6. What does the Psalm reading indicate?

Spend time praising God for His creative power.

Day 3: Psalm 8: Ex. 20:1-17; Rom. 1:18-20; 1:28 - 2:1 and 6:23

7. Explain the comparison between God and man.

8. From the Romans 6 reading, what hope is there for man?

9. Read Hebrews 1:1-3, and explain who Jesus Christ is and the gift He gave to us?

Spend time praising God for who He is. Agree with Him concerning yourself and any possible sins. Thank Him for His free gift through His Son Jesus Christ.

Day 4: John 3:1-21 and 4:5-29

10. A gift is only a gift when it is received without cost to the recipient. How then do we receive this free gift?

11. To receive this free gift, the woman at the well of Samaria had to recognize and accept some things about herself. She had to accept things about her upbringing, faith and the LORD Himself. What were they?

12.
   a. What is there in your own life that you need to accept?

   b. Have you done this?

Spend time talking to the LORD about any difficulties you may still have. Thank Him for His love and total control.

Day 5: Heb. 4:9-16; 11:1-3; 21-22 and 12:1-2

13. Lessons learned from Joseph and his family.

   a. What were the possible weights Joseph could have found which were easily besetting him?

   b. What were the possible weights his brothers may have struggled with?

    c.   What are the weights that so easily beset you?

14. Read Acts 9:1-22 (use a Biblical Dictionary if needed.) What does it mean to "kick against the pricks?" (You may need to look it up in a King James Bible.)

15. Can this ("kicking against the pricks") be a part of our lives even when we are Christians?

16. Summarise how Joseph had to be obedient during his life.

Spend time with God concerning any weights that easily beset you. Consider whether you have kicked against the leading and teaching of the LORD in your life...in any way!

Day 6

17. The following verses were previously used within the study of Joseph's life. From them, take time to consider and write down how each of us needs to be obedient in our daily lives.

Joshua 24:15

Palm 32:1-5

Proverbs 3:5-8

Proverbs 18:8

Matthew 10:28-32

Matthew 18:21 and 22

John 15:9-11

Acts 9:5 (KJV)

Philippians 4:4-6 and 8

Hebrews 3:19

Hebrews 4:10

Hebrews 4:15-16

1Peter 2:20-25

1Peter 3:15

1John 4:7-10

Spend time with the LORD; acknowledge any difficulties you may have in applying the Word of God in your life. Ask Him to give you the desire and strength to do so from here on, in order that He might receive all glory in your life.

Day 7: Final considerations. Gen. 47:1-12; 50:15-21 and Matt. 6:25-34

18. Did Jacob and his family want for anything when they were obedient and moved to Egypt?

19. Out of interest, which five brothers would you think Joseph presented to Pharaoh?

20. What does Matthew indicate concerning our needs?

21. Had Joseph's brothers forgiven themselves?

22. How do you think this would make God feel? Meditate on Psalm 103:11-12 and Colossians 2:13-15

Spend time with the LORD thanking Him for these spiritual truths and asking Him to help you walk daily within them, always learning to accept His will and way in your life. Ask Him to help you be obedient as unto the LORD, and to fill you with happiness and joy as you serve Him.

Lesson 6 Summary

Our journey with Joseph began with a dysfunctional family; a family without hope, chained by mistakes of the past, trapped by self-centredness, anger and resentment.

It began also with the question "What do You want me to learn, LORD?

As we've travelled this journey together, have you noted the changes in your life? Where did your journey begin? How far have you travelled?

We have discussed our need to accept many things, some of which have been:

- Our individuality and our responsibility for our own personal spiritual walk.

- Our sinfulness and our guilt and wretchedness before a holy and righteous God.

- Our need for repentance and obedience. The fact that we tend not to be spiritually minded, but instead have practised and grown to be earthly in mind and ways.

- Our inability to face up to the spiritual battle we are involved in, whether we like it or not.

- Our negligence in facing our Maker and acknowledging His right and authority over life and death, our needs and our problems.

- Our willingness to praise Him through these problems, so that He might receive all honour and glory in our lives; therefore, enabling Him to strengthen our faith even during difficult circumstances.

- Our need to come to the end of ourselves, completely, and in humility acknowledging own our mistakes before God; then in obedience laying them at the foot of the cross.

- Our understanding that God is to be our "hiding place" and the only One to whom we can turn.

But all these discoveries will be of no benefit if we neglect to make a definite decision to step out fully for God. Joshua 24:15b says:

> *"...choose you this day whom ye will serve whether the gods, which your fathers served, that were on the other side of the* river **(all part of your old way of life)** *or the gods of the Amorites* **(those of the world)**, *in whose land ye dwell; but as for me and my house, we will serve the LORD."*[69]
> **(Sections in bold and brackets added for clarity.)**

We have also discovered that we are always in a position of choice – moment-by-moment and day-by-day. No matter what the situation is, we have two ways we can travel; God's way or the completely opposite way that is directed by Satan, the world, self-centredness, heartache and sorrow.

We discovered also that our faith could only be built on a personal experience and knowledge of God. As we make our choice for Him, that knowledge increases. Remember it is not knowledge we can pass on, nor one gained from one's own intelligence, but one gained by simply stepping out in acceptance, obedience and prayerful experience of the grace and mercy of God.

Simply believing does not bring this experiential knowledge either, for James 2:19 reminds us:

> *"Thou believest that there is one God; thou doest well. The demons also believe and tremble."*[70]

No, it is a faith backed by action. One of total abandonment to God's loving care...in everything...always. It is coming to that place of recognition that "I" cannot do it and so I cease to strive in my own understanding and wisdom; cease to do my own works, and stop trying to do it my own way. This then is how we overcome the unbelief that troubles all of us. This is "dying to self." Jesus gave us the perfect example when He prayed:

> *"Father, if Thou be willing, remove this cup from me; nevertheless, not my will, but Thine, be done."* Luke 22:42[71]

No, life is not fair. It was unfair that Joseph should have had to live such a hard life, a life of sadness, heartache and sorrow, but his **acceptance and obedience** brought about the saving and preserving of a people for God. It brought about the healing within a family from which there seemed no way of escape.

It was not fair that Jesus Christ, God's Son, had to die for you and for me. However, His **acceptance and obedience** were so powerful, that it brought about the salvation of the world, of all who would turn to Him.

It is not fair that millions in this world have to go through such suffering. You may be one, but as you lean upon the One who has gone before and accept with love and grace in your heart that God has allowed this suffering for His glory and purpose: as you learn of Him, listen to and obey His commands, amidst all these sorrows…you too can be encouraged and filled with His love and presence.

Acknowledge that He is God: He knows, He controls, He leads and protects in the midst of sadness and in difficult times and He will fill us with His delight in being **"tools for service."** He will cleanse and forgive us and place us just where He wants to use us: wherever, whenever and however He should choose. For He alone must receive all the glory.

May we be complete in Him and delight in being His "tools for service"

Teacher's Manual

This study was designed for group Bible Study, but it can just as easily be used for individual use. It is advisable that if the latter is chosen, you make a point of finding yourself a faithful prayer warrior, someone you can trust and share your thoughts with. Sharing your thoughts often strengthens your resolve to cling to the truth. If in a group, remember to be a good leader, we must first learn to be a good listener. Be prepared to listen to the LORD. Do not fall into the trap of looking up the answers as you study. It is advisable to do this only when your own private study is completed. Also, be very willing to listen to those taking part within your group. The aim of this study is to draw each one of us closer to the LORD. Therefore, there will be a need to take time to listen. Be willing to share your own struggles and difficulties and be quick to stay silent when needed. Be careful not to fall into the same trap as Job's counsellors, who neglected to listen and thought they had all the answers. Be led by the LORD. A godly person once said; "we must not be led by the spirit of experience or the spirit of age, but rather by the Holy Spirit." You will need to be willing to pray, both throughout the week for each individual doing the study in your group and also during the study whenever it is needed.

It is also wise to encourage others to share. Many may not be used to doing so. Do not pressure them by asking them direct questions, unless this is acceptable to them all. You may find that sharing yourself or encouraging others to do so, breaks down any barriers. There may also be difficulties in getting some to pray aloud. Encourage them to do so by simple sentence prayers each week: this can help them to overcome their fear. Therefore, ensure that you do not pray long prayers, as this will only make it harder for them. Getting to know your members will give you knowledge as to how to lead. Encouraging others to read the sections in the book or Bible passages helps them to get used to the sound of their own voices.

Because this study can become quite personal, there will be some questions that some may prefer not to answer aloud. Be understanding and do not force the issue.

It can be very easy to be side tracked. Ensure that you hold the conversation in check if there is this tendency. Ensure that your group are aware of gossip and how easily this can spoil our fellowship and personal Christian walk. Each week before you part, pray that the LORD protects your conversation with others outside the group.

Be prepared to spend extra time with anyone that is in need. It is advisable to spend the first week going through the introduction and Background History.

May God bless you in your study.

TEACHER'S GUIDE

WEEK 1 The Dysfunctional Family accepting their own Sinfulness, yet God's Control.

Readings: - Gen. 37- 47:26

Day 1: Gen. 37:1-11; Matt 7:6; 10:28-32; Prov. 18:8 and 1Peter 3:15

1. He told tales about their evil doings (V 2)
   His father loved him more than the others, because he was the son of his old age and by his favourite wife. The position Jacob gave him was of the 'first-born' son; this affected everything (V 3)
   He had a dream indicating that there would be a time when they would all bow down to him. (V's 5-7)
   They felt that he was proud, thinking he would reign over them. (V 8)
   His second dream indicated all, (including his parents); the moon and stars, would bow down to him (V's 9-11)
   They were jealous of him. (V 11)

2. Here consider discernment and prayer. Some dealings are extremely personal. At times speaking with non-Christians is indeed *"giving that which is holy unto the dogs, or pearls to swine."* (Matt. 7:6)
   The goal here is for us to realise that Joseph wasn't always telling just how God was dealing with him. It is possible he had spiritual pride in his heart, certainly he told tales, which spoiled his witness. It is not our responsibility to correct others; especially close family members such as peers, husbands, wives and parents. Rather our goal should always be to love them, and be guided by the Holy Spirit. So always be ready

to share the hope that is in us, to stand up for our LORD, but not to proudly lord it over others. Note the position Jacob had given him was the first-born of his sons, (V 3) and how that would have affected all things

3. Ensure always to be humble: begin strengthening his relationship with God; and begin loving his brothers. Be careful of telling tales for the wrong reasons. This may not have made a difference to their relationship, but it certainly would have given God glory in Joseph's daily walk.

4.

   a. Yes, we should not fear man, but God. However, we must do so with God's wisdom, great kindness and precious love toward those we speak with: certainly, having no pride in our hearts!

   b. As God leads. Only God knows our family's hearts and needs; and as we depend on the leading of the Holy Spirit in our lives, He will always lead in the best way possible. Note the possibly suffering we may receive from doing so! (James 4:17; 1:14-15; 1John 3:4 and Rom. 14:23)

Day 2: Gen. 37:12-19 and Josh. 24:15

5. 17 years (V2).

6. This will be personal, be on the lookout for similar experiences that may need further time and prayer. If this is so, suggest a one to one meeting for some other time if needed.

7. When they began to feel jealous and hate him, and when they did not attempt to communicate their feelings to him in order to try to correct the situation.

8.

    a.   It is a simple act of will. As non-Christians we cannot prevent ourselves sinning; it is an automatic thing for mankind to sin, therefore help the class to see that as Christians we now do not have to sin. (Cf. also Rom. 6:11.)

    b.   (James 1:14, 15 and 4:17) explains that *"each of us is tempted when we are carried away and enticed by our own lust, then when lust has conceived, it gives birth to sin and when sin is accomplished, it brings forth death."* 4:17 says that *"when we know what to do and do not do it, that is sin."* (1John 3:4) tells us *"it is the transgression of the law."* Whilst (Rom. 14:23) reminds us *"that whatever is not of faith is sin.*

    c.   Satan, without salvation in our LORD Jesus Christ, mankind is bound in sin by the original fall in the Garden of Eden.

Day 3: Gen. 37; now re-read verses 20-36; John 15:25; Matt. 26:1-5; 14-25; 47-56; John 7:3-5 and Psalm 55:12-14

9.   Discussions will make sure your group are able to see that God was there with Joseph. This will be seen as the study progresses. Be aware that this may bring up sore spots, which need prayer.
Some suggestions may be:
His presence was overseeing what was happening.
He protected Joseph from death
There are no coincidences with God – He insured the Ishmaelites arrived at the right time; He organized Joseph's sale to Potiphar who seemed essentially a good man
He made sure of Joseph's training for His purposes, e.g. witnessing, preparation for leadership and the fulfillment of the dreams He had given Joseph.
He was in total control.

10. Personal discussion: consider these:

He could not fight God and it was time to trust Him completely with his future.

If the dreams were God speaking to his heart about the future, then there was to be a future.

Rest in Him and don't be fearful.

How to forgive his brothers!

Not to be proud of who he was, where he came from or how good he was.

Humility.

11. Their own brethren hated them both. Both were sold for the price of a slave, thirty pieces of silver. (20 shekels was at the time of Joseph the average price of a slave.)

Day 4: Gen. 39 and Jer. 29: 4-7

12. One who walked with God, with a godly attitude. Prosperous (V 2): note (So the Lord was with him.)

A righteous man, honourable: he loved God with all his heart and trusted Him in all aspects of his life.

A faithful and trustworthy servant!

One who respected his master greatly!

Handsome and well liked!

A good overseer!

13.

 a. That God was still in control and would never leave him (V15.)

Responsibility as a servant instead of as a master (V6.)

Responsibility as God's child, (for example – rules of conduct, loving God, others and himself, having a willingness to forgive others.) (V 8.)

A need to escape sexual pressure (V12.)

Injustice and suffering brought on by lies in life (V's 13-20.)

God's mercy (V 21.)

The loss of his family and to a degree his nationality.

To trust God in good and bad situations.
Obedience to God's righteousness.
Respect his masters.
Resting in God.

b. Yes: discuss.

c. Bitterness and resentment: anger towards God: No rest, no peace of mind as one tends to live in the flesh instead of the Spirit and therefore has a reactionary attitude to surrounding circumstance.

14.

a. This may differ with individuals, be willing to discuss. Be considerate, as there may be some very deep sorrows. Be prepared to pray.
    Consider some of the following:
    God is in control even when dreadful things happen.
    We must trust and love Him completely – walking always in the Spirit of God.
    Settle where we are placed, knowing God is with us and will never leave us.
    Rest in His love.
    Pray for those who persecute us.
    Do all in obedience for the LORD.
    Suffering will come, yet God is our strength.

b. Personal! Be willing to stop and pray together if needed.

Day 5: Gen. 40; Phil. 4: 11-13; 1Peter 2: 20-25; Isaiah 53 and Rom. 6: 3-19

15. This may be difficult to say. It may simply have been always a constant hope to escape his sorrows and return home. He may have been unconsciously trying to do God's work for Him. However, note his statement *"I was kidnapped from the land of the*

Hebrews." – there is no blame cast upon his brothers, which tends to show true forgiveness. Discuss!

16. God (V8). Note (V14) although, when we try to do God's job, we do not give Him glory!

17. He had learned (the secret) of being content and to know the strengthening of the LORD in difficult circumstances.

18. Take it patiently and follow the example of Christ Jesus. Help your group to remember the LORD, who was pure and undefiled, yet He suffered for us. He did it patiently without fighting for His rights. He did not threaten, but committed Himself to God who alone judges righteously.

Day 6: Gen. 41

19. Two full years passed. God knows the future and plans for it. He knows our troubles and sorrows; and uses circumstances to force even the slack to be obedient.

20. He gave God the glory for interpretations (V16.)
He said that the dream was from God (V's 25-36).
That God was revealing the future to Pharaoh, in order that they may prepare.
In the naming of his sons (V's 16, 25 and 28): Manasseh *"for God hath made me forget all my toil, and all my father's house"*; and Ephraim *"for God hath caused me to be fruitful in the land of my affliction."*

21. He recognised that the Spirit of God was in Joseph and that he was the only suitable man for the job (V's 38-44).
He showed great trust in him and he gave Joseph great authority
He was arrayed in fine linen and wore a gold chain about his neck.
He rode in Pharaoh's second chariot and all had to bow the knee before him.

Pharaoh also put his ring of power and authority on Joseph's finger.

22. God prepared him for the total fulfillment of his dreams of promise. By having him released from prison and placed second in charge under the King.

Day 7: Gen. 37: 5-11; and re-read Gen. 41: 33-36

23.

a. Maybe not. Often when used of God, it just happens. It's unlikely that God would bless him for the sin of pride. He would never have forgotten the dreams prior to 17 years old and now at 30 he would be assured of God's faithfulness, protection and perseverance – so he may have, but only as a depth of faith in the Almighty.

b. It would seem as a dream. He would simply praise God and his dreams would come back to mind. No doubt he would see how God used the sorrows to His glory and did not waste any.

WEEK 2 Accepting that Salvation and Security come from God Alone

Readings: - Gen. 42 and re-read 37

Day 1 Read Summary Notes

1. Discuss

2. Discuss

Day 2: Gen. 42; Gen. 37: 5-11; Matt. 18: 21-22; Psalm 32: 1-5 and Heb. 3:19

3. Yes. Discuss, consider these:
    His directing Joseph's ability to forgive and refrain from vengeance.
    How God brought the brothers to a place of repentance.
    God also brought them to the lands of Egypt and Canaan.
    He controlled the future.
    Joseph's dreams and the fulfilment of them.
    Jacob's grief, food, riches, and poverty.
    Because He is God, He knows the future and He keeps all His promises and continued to show His love to the family.

4. If needed, you can re-read Gen. 37: 5-10

5.

    a. Consider these:
    "Have they changed?
    Can I forgive them Lord?
    Can I trust them yet?
    Are they treating Benjamin the same way?
    I wonder just how Dad is?
    I wish none of this had ever come about, I know you have been in control God, but it brings such sadness to see how all this has come about.
    What action do I take from here on LORD?
    I love them so in spite of all this and they do need food."

    b. Absolute guilt.
    They felt they were being punished for their past sins.
    They may never see their families or friends again.
    What will happen to Dad? This will kill him, it's completely our fault!
    Anger at being accused wrongly in a strange country far from home.

Day 3: Gen. 42: 1-8; Rom. 1:18-23; 8:5-8; Luke 24: 13-32 and Heb. 3:19

6. Think about these:

   He would look older as twenty years had passed.

   He was dressed differently and spoke Egyptian.

   They were not prepared to ever see him again, probably thought he was dead: certainty not in a position of authority, maybe as a slave. They were hardened in the heart by unconfessed sin and so spiritually blinded.

   Note God's will and timing – the problem was they didn't know God.

7. Consider these:

   They were clouded with grief and sorrow.

   They were not spiritually minded, and so were not expecting to see Jesus alive, for they had seen Him crucified.

   They didn't think much of a woman's ability to deal with such things, and so they could not believe them concerning Jesus' resurrection.

   Their eyes were prevented from recognizing Him. (V16)

8. Discuss these possibilities:

   We can be carnally minded instead of spiritually.

   Taken up too much with the world's sphere, possibly carrying unconfessed sin and hardened hearts, so that unbelief troubles us.

9. No. Look up Rom. 8: 8 - 13

Day 4: Gen. 42: 1-28; Eccl. 3:1-8; Jonah 1: 17 and Luke 24: 19- 24

10. Discuss the feeling that he is being deceitful, versus the knowledge that God is in control. Note his harshness brings them to the end of themselves and helps them face their sin.

11.
    a. He wept and grieved

b. Discuss the possibility that he had not fully dealt with it and so had buried it.

Talk about the shock of his seeing family once again and the lost years with them.

Possibly struggling with an unforgiving bitter spirit toward them.

Thoughts of his father still being alive and Benjamin being grown and well.

The brother's guilty feelings and obvious remorse (V's 21, 22)

The knowledge of God's control.

c. Yes: Note, that we do not grieve as non- Christians do. We have a hope and therefore our faith in God must direct us to worship Him as in Job 1:21. Although, as Job discovered, and from personal experience I also learnt, it can be a struggle to keep on the godly track; for anger, loneliness and self-pity can direct us away from the LORD.

12. Two others:
Jonah in the big fish.
Jesus in the grave

13. The brothers needed to be forced into facing themselves and their sin, repentance was needed and acknowledgement of God's authority.

Joseph needed prayer time and a time to make sure he would be led by God: not anger or unforgiving towards them. However, he also felt a need to test them.

Jonah also needed to face his sin and the possibility of never having a chance to repent. He too needed to acknowledge God's authority.

Jesus had to fulfil His Father's will and the words He had said to the Jews and His disciples. Cf. Luke 11:29,30 and Matt. 28:5-7

Day 5: Gen. 42: 21-35; Rom. 2:1; 6:23 and Psalm 32 Q14 Simeon

14. Simeon

15. Themselves, each other and God. (21,22 and 28)

16. Personal. Consider the fact that it is natural for us to try and blame someone else. Note the Garden of Eden in (Genesis 3: 8-14)

17. Yes. To teach, correct and guide us. As a horse or mule has reins, so He too desires to lead us.

Day 6: Gen. 42: 35-38 and Rom. 8: 14-17

18. His sons

19. Accept God's total control and rest in Him without fear.

20. We have lost the spirit of bondage to fear and death. We have received the Spirit of adoption as children of God and Eternal life: giving us a wonderful inheritance in Christ Jesus.

Day 7: Psalm 32

21. Having our transgressions or sins forgiven: not just covered as in the OT, but blotted out – (Cf. Col 2:14 NASB) *"…having cancelled out the certificate of debt consisting of degrees against us."* Nothing is held against us, not because of who we are, but because of God's grace and mercy. When there is no deceit in our spirit, we are cleansed.

22. It affects us both spiritually and physically. We can end up feeling sick, depressed, and weighed down with guilt. All our happiness and joy disappear and we can be troubled night and day. One sin often leads to another.

23. God

24. Consider these:
    When trials and sorrows come upon us.
    When we have nowhere else to turn.
    For instruction, teaching and guidance.
    In confession and repentance.
    In happiness and rejoicing.
    Just to have a chat about EVERYTHING...ALWAYS.
    In 1Thess.5:17 we are encouraged to *"pray without ceasing."*

25. It is God alone who can protect us from trouble.
    He is our safety umbrella; nothing comes to us that hasn't first been
    filtered by Him.
    It is by Him in prayer that our thoughts are kept holy.
    We are taught, guided and instructed here.
    We are surrounded with songs of deliverance.
    It is here that we are compassed about with His great mercy and our
    hearts are turned from fear and sorrow to joy and rejoicing.
    For nothing can get to us.
    We are seated with Christ in Heavenly Places. (Eph.1:3

WEEK 3 Accepting that our walk must be one of faith

Reading: Genesis 43

Day 1: Read Summary notes.

1. Discuss

2. Personal, encourage those of your group to share if they are willing.

Day 2: Gen. 43; Prov. 3:5-8 and Gen. 49: 8-9

3. Help those of your study group to consider how God used the months to deal with Jacob's doubts and fears. Helping him to see that God and God alone, is the author of life and death. Jacob's fighting against God and the famine, which God controlled, would not protect his son Benjamin: far better to relinquish him, his love and himself into God's hands and see what happened. Note Gen. 49: 8-9 – the changing of his name shows faith (Israel) and God uses Judah to show true love and kindness allowing God to break the spirit of fear in (Jacob.)

4.
   a. No (V's 4,5) they lived with a fear of man. (V's 18-22) No rest in their hearts. They were unable to trust God and let Him fight the battles of life; instead they fought to justify themselves.

   b. Ch. 42:37 Ruben tries to change Jacob's mind by offering his sons to be killed if he didn't succeed.
   Ch.43:3-5 Judah, blames his Dad's fear and Joseph's sternness.
   Ch.43:18-22 They were afraid, thinking they would all become slaves. They kept striving to justify themselves.

   c. *"Trust in the Lord with all your heart and do not lean on your own understanding. In all your ways acknowledge Him, and He will make your paths straight."* Don't be wise in your own eyes; Fear the Lord and turn away from evil. It will be healing to your body and refreshment to your bones."

5.
   a. God. His faith was easily passed on, see (V23.)

   b. No. He had used the years to mould and make Joseph and prepare him for this day. While doing this He used him daily in the sharing of his faith in God.

6. Discuss the great need to grieve: the actual willingness to seek it and to be benefited from it, when the time is right. Note the fact that it can be a real healing time for us. Discuss whether it is wise in public, but the necessity in privacy. Make sure all acknowledge the damage that can be caused to them or their families by fighting it. Include the necessity to share your grief with God and allow Him to use it for His glory. (Grief is natural, but as Christians, we should not allow it to become self-pity. *"The LORD giveth and the LORD taketh away, blessed be the Name of the LORD."* Job. 1: 21)

Day 3: Gen. 42:29,36; 43:11; Acts 9: 1-20; 13: 9; 22: 1-16 and Acts 26: 9-18

7. (Cf. Gen. 32:28 and Gen. 35:10) Jacob = 'heel catcher' or 'deceiver': whilst Israel = 'God fighter' or 'he struggles with God'. Remind them that the name of Israel was given after his meeting with God. Discuss how meeting with God strengthens our faith. Note his attitude change from one of fear, anger and doubt to one of total abandonment to God and His power over life and death.

8. Re-read the Acts readings if needed. Discuss his anger and his willingness to stand by and watch as people were murdered. His willingness to have people put to death simply because they believed differently to him.

9. Ensure they know what it means to meet with the LORD. Discuss the fact that Paul realized that he could no longer fight against God or His truth. Note his acceptance of his own guilt before a Holy and Righteous God and his willingness to turn about in repentance and obedience.

10. Discuss the exact opposites of the answers in Q8. Note his peaceable quiet ways, his love for the brethren, his willingness to pray (V11). Note also that he was a man chosen by God, no longer spiritually blind with a willingness to obey God even in the waters of baptism: a man of faith.

Day 4: Hebrews 11

11. It is the end product of our hopes and the evidence or visible part of the unseen beliefs.

12. Read Heb. 11:6 *"Because without it, it is impossible to please God."*

13. That, *"He is God and that He rewards those who diligently seek Him"*

14. Jacob dwelt in tents with his father, (V9). Then in (V21) when he was dying he blessed his sons and worshiped the LORD leaning on the top of his staff.
    Joseph, when he was dying made mention of the exodus of the sons of Israel and gave orders concerning his bones (V22.)

15. Note the fact that when we least expect it, in God's eyes we are most faithful. It's the simple fuss-less faith in God that is important not the notable things we do for man. Also note both were most faithful at the point of death. (Cf. Rom. 6 in the aspect of dying to self). Also, the personal relationship they had with God, in order for Him to speak into their souls, both about death and future events – yet to be able to worship God.

Day 5: Gen 43: 11-15

16. Both – His acceptance was the working out of his faith.

17.
    a. faith = Complete confidence in a person or a plan; A strong belief in (a supernatural power) or God, who controls human destiny; and an institution to express belief in a divine power

    b. acceptance = The act of taking what is offered or given to one; The act of taking as true and satisfactory; belief; and a disposition to tolerance to accept situations.

Day 6: Gen. 43

18.

V1	The severity of the famine	everyone
V2	Egypt was the source of grain	Jacob & sons
V3,5	They could not return without Benjamin	Judah, brothers & Jacob
V4, 5	His sons' stubbornness	Jacob
V4, 5	The need for Benjamin to go.	Jacob
V6, 7	The ability to trust his sons with family in actions & words	Jacob
V8-10	He needed to take a responsible stand	Judah
V8-10	His life or death (future)	Judah
V11-14	He could no longer fight these previous facts	Israel
V14	That God Almighty had total control and only he could grant mercy	Israel
V14	Death and separation was in God's hands also	Israel
V17	That Joseph was his boss and he was simply a servant	Joseph's servant
V18-22	They were not in control	the brothers
	They were afraid	the brothers
	They may end up as slaves	the brothers
	They may be deemed as liars and thieves	the brothers
	They needed mercy	the brothers
V23	He had a faith & assurance to share	the servant
V24	He had responsibilities and work to do	the servant
V25	They were invited for a meal	the brothers
V26	Joseph was indeed in authority over them	the brothers
V30	He had a need to grieve	Joseph

V31	The need to control himself	Joseph
V32	The cultural difference	Joseph, Egyptians & brothers
V34	Joseph knew the order of their ages.	the brothers

Many of these may seem trivial, but each can relate to our lives if we think about them; encourage everyone to discuss fully.

19. This will be personal, but encourage all to share their thoughts, and if none are forth coming you may consider these:
    a. The stubbornness of family members
    b. The need for hard things that have to come about and following through with them.
    c. The ability to trust family members for example: – your spouse with the discipline of the children; with each other's emotions and feelings, (both speech & actions); your spouse and children with their responsibilities and parents with understanding and loving words.
    d. The need to be responsible and reliably for example: – remembering to do tasks we are asked to specifically do by our spouse or parents, no matter how minor it may seem to be to us.
    e. That God alone is in control of life and death.
    f. We can't fight God.
    g. Only God can be trusted to be merciful.
    h. That He is the Almighty.
    i. Our position as men and women and our roles as such.
    j. We can't always be in control.
    k. Fear is a natural emotion and only God can strengthen us during these times.
    l. God is in control of the future.
       We may not always be understood.
    m. We are all in need of God's mercy.
    n. As Christians, we have a faith and assurance to share; this is a responsibility.
    o. We need to happily fulfil our work and roles in life.

p. We need to go to Jesus for mercy and He will feed us with His grace.

q. Jesus Christ our Lord has all authority over us.

r. There is a need to grieve at certain times in life, over loss of family members. Loss of physical abilities. Sometimes over children's waywardness. Certainly, over any sorrows, which weigh us down.

s. There is a need for SELF-CONTROL, prior to SELF-PITY.

t. There is a cultural difference within our countries, we should accept others and love them as Jesus Christ does.

u. Wherever we are and whatever is happening in our lives, Jesus Christ both knows and has gone before us.

v. Our rewards are all to be different. God has the right to choose what reward we should get, for He alone is God.

Day 7: Gen. 43; Heb. 11: 1-3 and Rom. 10: 17

20.
V3-5	Judah & brothers	They did not go without Benjamin
V11-14	Israel	He was obedient in sending Benjamin
V15	The brothers	They obeyed their father
V17, 24	Joseph's servant	He obeyed Joseph.

21. This is personal. You may need to spend time in prayer. Have a listening ear if needed and a compassionate heart.

22.

a. We must accept that God is God, only then can faith be born. Faith is the maturity of a learned knowledge and acceptance of God. It is the belief that God is in control of our past, present and future and that He cares about us. Therefore, we can rest in Him and talk with Him over our daily concerns. Acceptance is the working out of our faith.

b. Discuss

WEEK 4 The family accepted that it was chosen and therefore needed to be set apart for God.

Readings: Genesis 44,37 and 49

Day 1: Read Summary Notes.

1. The act of taking what is offered or given to one; the act of taking as true and satisfactory; belief; or approval and the act or disposition to tolerate or accept a situation.

2. Encourage all to share.

3. Personal, but do encourage those who wish to share their thoughts and prayers.

Day 2: Gen. 37:20-36; Gen. 44: 1-7 and verses 27b-34

4. Consider this:
    The brothers had previously shown great hatred for the son who was the object of their father's love.
    Did he feel he needed to know that this was not going to be the case now with Benjamin as well?
    Joseph was making sure that they had faced themselves. Note the words in (Ch. 44:4b) *"why have you repaid evil for good?"* It was a question that would remind them of what they had done to Joseph all those years ago. What they had done to Jacob – causing such sorrow throughout his life.

5. Yes, they now accepted their father's love for Benjamin and both loved him and their father and showed great respect. Probably watching Jacob's severe grief over the loss of Joseph would have left them with guilt, which they too could not change. However, these

things can drive us to be better people – equally they can also cause us to give up and become worse: the choice is ours.

Day 3: Gen: 44:1-13; 43:23; 1Peter 3:1 and Eph. 5: 22-33

6. There is no indication that this was so, however, it may lead to lively discussion.

7. Yes, He obviously had a deep faith both in Joseph and his God. He had the heart of his master. He may have felt this action a little hypocritical, but he had watched Joseph's reaction throughout the brother's visits and must have realized something different was going on. He had learned to trust his master.

8. No, but this may be too personal; help them to accept the differences between themselves and those in authority over them. At times we do not want to understand – *"the heart is desperately wicked who can know it"* (Jer. 17: 9.) At times we have hidden agendas and simply prefer to do our own thing, this gives us a hardened heart, which is unable to understand! Then again those in authority do not always give their reasons nor should they have to! Past hurts sometimes cause us to find it hard to trust and obey those in authority! Be prepared to pray through.

9. Personal. This could be easily opened up for discussion and possibly prayer.

Day 4: Gen. 44: 14-17; Gen. 37: 5-11 and Heb. 4:12,13.

10. The fulfilment of Joseph's dream. They were fully bowing down to him, accepting his power over them and begging for mercy. We have a Sovereign God who knows our future and our sins.

11. That he had the ability not only to know but also to find out what he didn't know. God has given me discernment, I have power over you. It's time to except the fulfillment of my dreams. This is a picture of God.

12. That He knows our hearts. The Word of God, who is Christ, is living and active. His Holy Spirit sees every nook and cranny; He divides between the soul and spirit of each of us. He judges both our thoughts and intentions of the heart. No creature is hidden from His sight; in fact, all are laid bare and open before Him.

13. The righteousness of God who knows all their sins – past and present. He had revealed this to them fully and that they were now all the slaves of Joseph.

Day 5: Gen. 44:18-34 and Gen. 37:20-36

14. No, but he probably was more upright in being willing to take Benjamin's place of servitude and he does show a genuine love for his father. He earlier showed he had no desire to shed his brother's blood – even as Reuben didn't, but he willingly suggested making money out of selling him as a slave.

15. He was the fourth son of Leah and Jacob. His name means, "praise Jehovah."

Day 6: Gen. 44:16-34; Heb. 4:12-16; 10: 31; Rom. 3:23 and 6:23

16. To call upon Joseph's mercy (V20)! 'You asked, we obeyed, Jacob loved – please give mercy?' To keep his father alive, he was willing to take Benjamin's punishment and so set him free.

17. No. Possibly he thought he did: because Joseph loved Benjamin completely and as the one in control, he had organized the whole situation.

    Yes. For the brother's sake: they were unaware of the hidden truths. They needed to be up front and honest. They needed to accept God's righteousness and their own wickedness.

18. Yes. We are wretched before a Holy and Righteous God. Even though God loved us while we were still sinners, we were unaware of His great love. It has been through His Son's sacrifice and intercession for us that we begin to recognize His Holiness, His love and our own hopelessness before Him. Even when we are most holy Isaiah 64:6 reminds us compared to God's Holiness, we are just like "filthy rags."

19. Jesus Christ, God's Son (Heb. 7:24, 25)

Day 7: Gen. 49: 1-28: (NIV or NASB use may be wise.); Heb.7: 14; 11:21, 22 and Matt. 1:1-3; extra reading Gen. 35:22

20. He was unstable then too. Knowing what they were doing was wrong, trying to prevent death, but still easily led into sin simply because he didn't stand firm for what was right. Earlier in life he showed himself sexually promiscuous, he slept with Bilhah, his father's concubine.

21. Jacob describes him as an angry man. Maybe as the second eldest he was the ringleader. It's possible that if he was, Joseph preferred to remove him from the family, hoping that truth and justice would prevail.

22. His brothers would always praise him. He would take hold of his enemies by the neck, thus preventing them from bringing about death to the Israelites. He was the son of a lion; therefore, he is discerning, wise and strong: the one with authority to rule. The

people will obey him. He has the riches and power. He is the intercessor and symbolic of Messiah – our true intercessor who was born through Judah's tribe.

23. He obeyed the Father's will and became our substitute in separation from God, He carried God's entire wrath, which was meant for us and took the punishment of death, even though He was without sin.

WEEK 5 Accepting True Healing Readings:

Reading: Genesis 45

Day 1: Read Summary Notes.

1. Personal, encourage those of your group to share their new thoughts.

2. You may desire to pray, praising God for the lessons learnt.

Day 2: Gen. 45: 1-3; Ex. 20: 1-17; Rom. 3:23 and Phil. 2: 9-11

3. Joseph is now 39 and had been separated from his family for 22 years, (Cf. Gen. 37:2). They were terrified at his presence (V3)
   They had really never thought to see him alive again.
   Joseph had spoken Egyptian and therefore used an interpreter.
   As well as this he had proved to them a hard taskmaster – not their brother.
   They may have suddenly begun to wonder what he would do to punish them.

4. Consider the fact that their guilt would be excessively great at this time. They knew that Joseph knew their hidden sins and as the one in authority, they also knew his power of life and death over them.

5. They needed to confess and ask his forgiveness, mercy and grace. Then be aware of the knowledge of his forgiveness – they also had to meet or have a revelation of God's love.

6.

    a. At His Name, *"every knee should bow, of things in heaven and things in earth and things under the earth. And that every tongue should confess that Jesus Christ is Lord, to the glory of God, the Father."* (V10 and 11.) (KJV)

    b. No, not yet, this is for a future fulfilment.

Day 3. Gen. 45: 1-8 and Heb. 4: 14-16

7. Yes, because of the LORD's sacrifice for us.

8. Because of their sin against him and his power over them; however, they knew God's judgement also (Cf. Gen. 42: 21,22).

9. John 3: 16-21...Unbelief: preferring the dark things of life and so being condemned. The fact that our sins will be made clear to us as we come near to the light of God causes mankind to prefer darkness rather than light.
    Psalm 32: 3-5...Unconfessed sin.
    Psalm 66:18...If we regard any wickedness or wrongdoing {sin} in our hearts, God will not hear us.
    Isaiah 59:2...Our iniquities separate us from Him and our sins hide His face from us, that He will not hear us.
    2Tim. 3:5...Having a form of godliness, but not really being saved and so denying the power of salvation: being hypocritical.
    1Tim. 4:7b ...Not exercising ourselves in the way of godliness. Being lazy and so not bothering to spend time with the LORD.

10.

    a.   He was sent there by God to preserve the life of his family.

    b.   Because this is where God has placed us and we are here for His purposes and glory.

Day 4: Gen. 45: 1-8; Rom. 8: 28-39 and Rom. 11:5

11. *"That all things work together for good to them that love God, to them who are the called according to His purpose. For whom He did foreknow, He also predestined to be conformed to the image of His Son."* (KJV)

12. Five (V6)

13. He was preserving a remnant in Egypt through Joseph's aid and protection (V7).

14. Personal. Be prepared if needed, to share some hard things in your life to assist the others to open up and share. This may be a good time to spend in prayer. Be specific and don't draw it out as this could bring your meeting to a close for the day.

Day 5: Gen. 45: 1-15; Matt. 26: 28; 1John 4: 7-10 and John 15: 9-11

15. He had brought on the famine.
He had fully informed Pharaoh and Joseph, enabling them to prepare.
He had kept them through the last two years and was going to keep them in the following five.
He had sent Joseph to Egypt and allowed all the heartaches that he had endured to train him.
He had saved Joseph's family by a great deliverance.
He helped Joseph forgive his brothers and so enabled him not to waste his sorrows.

He made him a father to Pharaoh and lord of his entire house and a ruler throughout Egypt.

He restored Joseph both to his family and with his family.

16. Personal. Do encourage all to see the everyday things God has done, such as sustaining and keeping, but remind them also of their salvation and hope. It may also be a worthy thing to encourage them to thank Him for the hard knocks in life.

17. Personal. Encourage them to re-think the answers of previous questions.

Day 6: Gen. 45 16-20

18.
    a. It pleased him well and his servants

    b. By this stage they loved Joseph, they recognised him for his love and justice. He had a relationship with his God that was real. This brought blessing to both him and those surrounding him. Possibly they thought the family would do the same. There is no mention of Pharaoh knowing how Joseph originally arrived in Egypt. Note (Gen. 40:15) Joseph has never cast blame on his brothers, which shows true forgiveness.

19. Load their beasts, go to Canaan, get their families and bring them back to eat the good of the land. Take our wagons for your little ones. Also leave all possessions behind for the good of the land of Egypt is theirs.

Day 7: Gen. 45:16-28; Phil. 3:13,14 and 2Cor. 5: 17-21

20. It was a complete life change, leaving the land promised to Abraham to go to Egypt. Discuss things such as leaving all they knew and

were comfortable with, even possessions such as furniture. Coping with a new culture different to their own, for example – their eating habits: a different language and different ways. The possible "what ifs"– Joseph or present Pharaoh dies for example.

21.

    a.   Because Israel loved Joseph and he also wanted his family united; however, more importantly he had come to a place of faith and knew God's leading in the move.

    b.   Because we love Him: He has reconciled us unto Himself and forgiven us all things through Christ Jesus our Lord.

22. *"Forgetting those things which are behind…I press toward the mark for the prize of the high calling of God in Christ Jesus."* (KJV) Thank Him for reconciliation and step out in the ministry He has given us, that of helping others to be also reconciled to God. Live to His glory in life as a new creation, put away all the trappings of the old life, recognizing they are no longer to be part of our lives.

WEEK 6 Learning from Joseph and his family

Day 1: Gen. 45: 21-28; Mark 9: 14-29 and Mark 16:1-14

1. Jacob = 'heel catcher or deceiver'
Israel = 'God's fighter or he struggles with God' (Cf. Gen. 32:28 & 35: 10)
When struggling with belief or faith, he is always referred to as Jacob. However, when his faith is restored by God's grace, he is always called Israel.

2. Yes, it appears that seeing with their own eyes helped them to believe, otherwise it always seemed too good to be true. Note that with personal experience, we too can be stronger in faith. Discuss

what sort of faith this may be. Is it faith in God, or simply trusting our own experiences?

3. *"LORD, I believe; help thou mine unbelief."* The NIV says, *"I do believe, help me overcome my unbelief!"*

> There may be a need for you to glance over your questions and answers from the previous weeks.

Day 2: Gen. 1:1; John 1; Psalm 139:13-16

4. The goal here is to help each person understand that God is God and thank Him for His creation.

5. There is no really wrong answer here, as it is pure supposition, but consider in the pit, in prison, or during his down times.

6. That God also made us, He was there when we were being formed in our mother's womb and He wrote all our members down in His book: we were fearfully and wonderfully made.

Day 3: Psalm 8; Ex. 20: 1-17; Rom. 1: 18-20; 1: 28-2:1 and Rom. 6:23

7. It is desirable here that all would be able to see the difference between Holy and unholy, Righteous and unrighteous. To see our absolute hopelessness before a Holy and Righteous God who has the right to punish us with great wrath; but instead chooses to pour out His love upon us.

8. We have a free gift given to us from God, through our Lord Jesus Christ: that of salvation.

9. Ensure each person is able to see that truly Jesus Christ is God come in the flesh, sent from the Father. He is Holy and righteous even as the Father is and the only one who is suitable as a sacrifice for us. The gift was dying for us. To purge means, "to make clean and purify." *"Who being the brightness of His glory"* can be translated (Who being not a reflection, but the light itself); and brightness= effulgence, radiance or splendour. Therefore, He is the exact representation of the Father. Through Him is the only way we can get to know our Heavenly Father.

Day 4: John 3: 1-21 and 4: 5-29

10. Discuss being "born again." It is the act of belief; accepting that you cannot do it, only God can and turning to Him through His Son and saying thank you for His free gift. Baptism does not save us; it is the outward showing of what has already taken place within our souls. However, as we are lowered into the water by full emersion, it reminds us that we have decided to die to ourselves, sin and death: then as we are raised up out of the water we are reminding ourselves that we have been risen again in Christ Jesus – thus "born again." Truly it is spiritual and not physical as Jesus told Nicodemus.

11. She had to recognize her need and sin: facing up to it before God. She also had to tell the LORD the barriers within her upbringing (their belief system, which was not accurate.) She also had to recognize that the LORD was her only hope and was indeed the Messiah they had long awaited.

12.
    a. Personal. Be aware that there may be a need to pray specifically for some.
        Consider some things such as being born who you are; our ages; our families and upbringing.
        Consider a difficult marriage or rebellious children.

Consider also things we may feel are personality or physical defects.

b. Personal. Please encourage those who are willing to share their thoughts if they can, but don't push the issue.

Day 5: Heb. 4: 9-16; 11: 1-3, 21-22 and 12: 1-2

13.
a. Depression; sexual desires; pride; anger; bitterness and resentment.

b. Guilt; depression; pride; anger and resentment.

c. Much of this is personal, but discussion can be had concerning Joseph and his brothers. Be aware that some may require a one to one due to concerns in their lives. If this is needed, make an appointment to spend quality time with them in prayer.

14. A goad or prick was a sharp piece of metal attached to a seven-foot long stick. This was used to direct the oxen in the way the farmer wished them to go. Here, Jesus was saying, "I have been trying to direct your life, but you keep rebelling against my directions."

15. Yes, we must be prepared to 'die to self'. Discuss this in full.

16. Consider the sins of pride, resentment and the inability to forgive that he would need to repent from. Consider also his need to be content, not to worry about his loved ones or his future. Consider also his daily walk, being subservient.

Day 6:

17. Joshua 24:15   We need to choose daily, moment by moment who we will serve.

Psalm 32: 1-5	Confess your own sin, forgive yourself and accept God's forgiveness.
Prov. 3: 5-8	*"Trust in the Lord with all your heart and lean not on your own understanding. Acknowledge Him in all your ways".*
Prov. 18:8	Don't be a talebearer.
Matt. 10:28-32	Fear not the world, or the devil, but have a righteous fear of God who is alone able to destroy both soul and body in hell. We are more valuable than many sparrows.
Matt. 18:21,22	Be ready always to forgive, over and over again. Ask God for help in this.
John 15:9-11	Keep His commandments and continue in His love. Be at one with Christ, even as He is with the Father.
Acts 9:5	Don't kick against God's directing of our lives.
Phil. 4:4,6 and 8	Rejoice always; be gentle to all men; don't worry – just pray and think on true, honest, just, pure, lovely, well-reported, virtuous and praiseworthy things.
Heb. 3:19	Make sure there is no unbelief in our hearts. Help all to understand the inability to enter into God's rest (see Chapter 4), which always indicates that unbelief is present.
Heb. 4:10	Stop trying to do God's job for Him, for this is doing all in our own strength.
Heb. 4:15-16	Remember always that we have a great High Priest who has gone before us; and so, go boldly into His throne of grace.
1Peter 2:20-25	Be willing to suffer and do it patiently, knowing this is acceptable to God. Follow the example of our LORD: this enables us to die to self and live to righteousness.
1Peter 3:15	Sanctify, (set apart), the LORD God in your hearts, and be always ready to share the faith God has given you.

1John 4:7-10   Be born of God, know His love and always love one another

Day 7: Final Considerations: - Gen. 47: 1-12; 50: 15-21 and Matt. 6:25-34

18. No

19. We are of more importance than the fowls of the air to God. He supplies their needs and He will do so for us also. Worrying about our needs is an aspect that the unbeliever will have as part of their lives; it should not be part of ours. Instead we should always endeavour to *"seek first the kingdom of God and His righteousness"* and all our needs will be supplied.

20. No, this shows by their fear of Joseph when their Dad passed away.

21. It would sadden His heart, for when He forgives He remembers no more.

BIBLIGROPHY

1   The New Scofield Reference Bible, (Authorized KJV) C.I. Scofield, D.D.; Oxford University Press, New York 1967., (Pg. 1299, 1Tim. 4:7b.)

2   The New Scofield Reference Bible, (Authorized KJV) C.I. Scofield, D.D.; Oxford University Press, New York 1967., (Pg.1242, 1 Cor.10:11.)

3   The New Scofield Reference Bible, (Authorized KJV) C.I. Scofield, D.D.; Oxford University Press, New York 1967., (Pg.25, Gen. 17:5), ('m'; sub. chain ref.)
    The Genesis Record, Commentary; by Morris, Henry M.; Baker Book House, Grand Rapids, Michigan, USA.; Master Books, El Cajon, California, USA; 1976 thirteenth printing 1988., Pg. 332, paragraph 3, line 2.

4   The New Scofield Reference Bible, (Authorized KJV) C.I. Scofield, D.D.; Oxford University Press, New York 1967., (Pg.25, Gen.17:5), ('l'; sub. chain ref.)

5   The New Scofield Reference Bible, (Authorized KJV) C.I. Scofield, D.D.; Oxford University Press, New York 1967., (Pg.25, Gen.17:1.)

6   The New Scofield Reference Bible, (Authorized KJV) C.I. Scofield, D.D.; Oxford University Press, New York 1967., (Pg.26, Gen. 17:19), ('k' sub. chain ref.)

7   The New Scofield Reference Bible, (Authorized KJV) C.I. Scofield, D.D.; Oxford University Press, New York 1967., (Pg.32, Ch 22:1-14.)

8   Strong's Exhaustive Concordance of the Bible; Strong, James, S.T.D., L.L.D. Thomas Nelson Publishers Inc., Nashville, Tennessee 37203 ('lad', Pg.578/79, Heb. Dict. 5288)

9   The New Scofield Reference Bible, (Authorized KJV) C.I. Scofield, D.D.; Oxford University Press, New York 1967., (Pg.32, Ch.22:6.) (notes)

10 The New Scofield Reference Bible, (Authorized KJV) C.I. Scofield, D.D.; Oxford University Press, New York 1967., (Pg.33, Gen.23:1.) (gives Sarah's age when she died- 127: Isaac was born when she was -90)

11 The New Scofield Reference Bible, (Authorized KJV) C.I. Scofield, D.D.; Oxford University Press, New York 1967., (Pg.38, Ch.26:1-5.)

12 The New Scofield Reference Bible, (Authorized KJV) C.I. Scofield, D.D.; Oxford University Press, New York 1967., (Pg.38, Ch. 25:26), ('b' sub. chain ref.)

13 The New Scofield Reference Bible, (Authorized KJV) C.I. Scofield, D.D.; Oxford University Press, New York 1967., (Pg. 39-42, Ch. 27-28.)

14 The New Scofield Reference Bible, (Authorized KJV) C.I. Scofield, D.D.; Oxford University Press, New York 1967., (Pg.45-47, Ch.31.)

15 The New Scofield Reference Bible, (Authorized KJV) C.I. Scofield, D.D.; Oxford University Press, New York 1967., (Pg.43, Ch29:32.) ('g' sub. chain ref.)

16 The New Scofield Reference Bible, (Authorized KJV) C.I. Scofield, D.D.; Oxford University Press, New York 1967., (Pg. 51, Ch. 35:22.)

17 The New Scofield Reference Bible, (Authorized KJV) C.I. Scofield, D.D.; Oxford University Press, New York 1967., (Pg.68, Ch 49:3-4.)

18 The New Scofield Reference Bible, (Authorized KJV) C.I. Scofield, D.D.; Oxford University Press, New York 1967., (Pg.43, Ch. 29:33), ('i' sub. chain ref.)

19 The New Scofield Reference Bible, (Authorized KJV) C.I. Scofield, D.D.; Oxford University Press, New York 1967., (Pg.68, Ch. 49:5-7.)

20 The New Scofield Reference Bible, (Authorized KJV) C.I. Scofield, D.D.; Oxford University Press, New York 1967., (Pg.43, Ch 29:34), ('k' sub. chain ref.)

21 The New Scofield Reference Bible, (Authorized KJV) C.I. Scofield, D.D.; Oxford University Press, New York 1967., (Pg. 43, Ch 29:35), ('l' sub. chain ref.)

22 The New Scofield Reference Bible, (Authorized KJV) C.I. Scofield, D.D.; Oxford University Press, New York 1967., (Pg. 68, Ch. 49:8b-9a.)

23 The New Scofield Reference Bible, (Authorized KJV) C.I. Scofield, D.D.; Oxford University Press, New York 1967., (Pg.44, Ch.30:18), ('a' sub. chain ref.)

24 The New Scofield Reference Bible, (Authorized KJV) C.I. Scofield, D.D.; Oxford University Press, New York 1967., (Pg. 69, Ch.49:14-15.)

25 The New Scofield Reference Bible, (Authorized KJV) C.I. Scofield, D.D.; Oxford University Press, New York 1967., (Pg. 44, Ch.30:20), ('b' sub chain ref.)

26 The New Scofield Reference Bible, (Authorized KJV) C.I. Scofield, D.D.; Oxford University Press, New York 1967., (Pg. 43, Ch 30:6), ('p' sub chain ref.)

27 The New Scofield Reference Bible, (Authorized KJV) C.I. Scofield, D.D.; Oxford University Press, New York 1967., (Pg. 69, Ch. 49:16-18.)

28 The New Scofield Reference Bible, (Authorized KJV) C.I. Scofield, D.D.; Oxford University Press, New York 1967., (Pg. 43, Ch. 30:8), ('q' sub chain ref.)

29 The New Scofield Reference Bible, (Authorized KJV) C.I. Scofield, D.D.; Oxford University Press, New York 1967., (Pg. 69, Ch. 49:21).

30 The New Scofield Reference Bible, (Authorized KJV) C.I. Scofield, D.D.; Oxford University Press, New York 1967., (Pg. 43, Ch.30:11), ('s' sub chain ref.)
    The Genesis Record, Commentary; by Morris, Henry M.; Baker Book House, Grand Rapids, Michigan, USA.; Master Books, El Cajon, California, USA; 1976 thirteenth printing 1988. (Pg. 467, Par. 3, Line 3)

31 The New Scofield Reference Bible, (Authorized KJV) C.I. Scofield, D.D.; Oxford University Press, New York 1967., (Pg. 69, Ch.49:19).
    The Genesis Record, Commentary; by Morris, Henry M.; Baker Book House, Grand Rapids, Michigan, USA.; Master Books, El Cajon, California, USA; 1976 thirteenth printing 1988. (Pg. 467, Par. 3, Line 3)

32 The New Scofield Reference Bible, (Authorized KJV) C.I. Scofield, D.D.; Oxford University Press, New York 1967., (Pg. 43 Ch.30:13), ('t' sub. chain ref.)
    The Genesis Record, Commentary; by Morris, Henry M.; Baker Book House, Grand Rapids, Michigan, USA.; Master Books, El Cajon, California, USA; 1976 thirteenth printing 1988. (Pg. 467, Par. 3, Line 3)

33 The New Scofield Reference Bible, (Authorized KJV) C.I. Scofield, D.D.; Oxford University Press, New York 1967., (Pg. 44, Ch. 30:24), ('g' sub. chain ref.)

34 The New Scofield Reference Bible, (Authorized KJV) C.I. Scofield, D.D.; Oxford University Press, New York 1967., (Pg.53, Ch. 37:3-4), (Pg. 69, Ch. 49:22-26).

35 The New Scofield Reference Bible, (Authorized KJV) C.I. Scofield, D.D.; Oxford University Press, New York 1967., (Pg. 51, Ch. 35:18) ('2' notes)

36 Adapted from the Genesis Record, Commentary; by Morris, Henry M.; Baker Book House, Grand Rapids, Michigan, USA.; Master Books, El Cajon, California, USA; 1976 thirteenth printing 1988. (Pg. 557, par. 5, lines 1-3).

37 Adapted from the Genesis Record, Commentary; by Morris, Henry M.; Baker Book House, Grand Rapids, Michigan, USA.; Master Books, El Cajon, California, USA; 1976 thirteenth printing 1988. (Pg. 559, Par. 1.)

38 The New Scofield Reference Bible, (Authorized KJV) C.I. Scofield, D.D.; Oxford University Press, New York 1967., (Pg. 767, Ch.64:6)"

39 NASB-NIV Parallel New Testament in Greek and English with Interlinear: Marshall, Alfred. Regency Reference Library; Zondervan Publishing House, Grand Rapids, Michigan. USA. 1987. (Pg. 687, 1 John 3:1 NASB)

40 NASB-NIV Parallel New Testament in Greek and English with Interlinear: Marshall, Alfred. Regency Reference Library; Zondervan Publishing House, Grand Rapids, Michigan. USA. 1987. (Pg. 691, 1 John 4:10 NASB)

41 NASB-NIV Parallel New Testament in Greek and English with Interlinear: Marshall, Alfred. Regency Reference Library; Zondervan Publishing House, Grand Rapids, Michigan. USA. 1987. (Pg. 564, Eph. 4:22-27 NASB)

42 NASB-NIV Parallel New Testament in Greek and English with Interlinear: Marshall, Alfred. Regency Reference Library; Zondervan Publishing House, Grand Rapids, Michigan. USA. 1987. (Pg. 568/9, Eph. 6:10-18a NASB)

43 The New Compact Bible Dictionary: Pillar Books for Zondervan Publishing House, Grand Rapids, Michigan 1967, 24th print 1978, (Pg.423)
The Exhaustive Dictionary of Bible Names: Cornwall, Judson Th. D., D.D. and Smith, Stelman M.M., M.TH., TH. D.; Bridge-Logos Publishers, Nth Brunswick, NJ. USA:(Pg. 196)

44 The New Scofield Reference Bible, (Authorized KJV) C.I. Scofield, D.D.; Oxford University Press, New York 1967., (Pg. 1235, 1 Cor. 3:1a)

45 NASB-NIV Parallel New Testament in Greek and English with Interlinear: Marshall, Alfred. Regency Reference Library; Zondervan Publishing House, Grand Rapids, Michigan. USA. 1987. (Pg.485, 1 Cor.3:3)

46 NASB-NIV Parallel New Testament in Greek and English with Interlinear: Marshall, Alfred. Regency Reference Library; Zondervan Publishing House, Grand Rapids, Michigan. USA. 1987. (Pg. 657, James 1:13-15)

47 NASB-NIV Parallel New Testament in Greek and English with Interlinear: Marshall, Alfred. Regency Reference Library; Zondervan Publishing House, Grand Rapids, Michigan. USA. 1987. (Pg. 656/7, James 1:2-6 and v.8)

48 NASB-NIV Parallel New Testament in Greek and English with Interlinear: Marshall, Alfred. Regency Reference Library; Zondervan Publishing House, Grand Rapids, Michigan. USA. 1987. (Pg. 657, James 1:12)

49 The MacArthur Study Bible: MacArthur, John; NASB, Thomas Nelson Inc, 2006, (Pg.757, Psalm 32:7)

50 The New Scofield Reference Bible, (Authorized KJV) C.I. Scofield, D.D.; Oxford University Press, New York 1967., (Pg. 1314, Heb. 4:10.)

51 The New Scofield Reference Bible, (Authorized KJV) C.I. Scofield, D.D.; Oxford University Press, New York 1967., (Pg. 1314, Heb. 4:6)

52 The New Scofield Reference Bible, (Authorized KJV) C.I. Scofield, D.D.; Oxford University Press, New York 1967., (Pg.1314, Heb. 4:11)

53 The MacArthur Study Bible: MacArthur, John; NASB, Thomas Nelson Inc, 2006, (Pg. 583, 1 Chron. 28:9)

54 Strong's Exhaustive Concordance of the Bible; Strong, James, S.T.D., L.L.D. Thomas Nelson Publishers Inc., Nashville, Tennessee 37203. ('know' Pg.574/47, Heb. Dict. 3045)

55 The New Scofield Reference Bible, (Authorized KJV) C.I. Scofield, D.D.; Oxford University Press, New York 1967., (Pg. 61, Gen. 43:14)

56 The MacArthur Study Bible: MacArthur, John; NASB, Thomas Nelson Inc, 2006, (Pg. 583, 1 Chron. 28:9a)

57 The New Scofield Reference Bible, (Authorized KJV) C.I. Scofield, D.D.; Oxford University Press, New York 1967., (Pg. 1344, I John 3:1a)

58 The MacArthur Study Bible: MacArthur, John; NASB, Thomas Nelson Inc, 2006, (Pg. 1791/2, Phil. 2:6-8)

59 The MacArthur Study Bible: MacArthur, John; NASB, Thomas Nelson Inc, 2006, (Pg. 1938, 1 John 3:1a)

60 The New Scofield Reference Bible, (Authorized KJV) C.I. Scofield, D.D.; Oxford University Press, New York 1967., (Pg. 624, Psalm 51:3-4)

61 NASB-NIV Parallel New Testament in Greek and English with Interlinear: Marshall, Alfred. Regency Reference Library; Zondervan Publishing House, Grand Rapids, Michigan. USA. 1987. (Pg. 640/1, Heb. 9:1 and 6-10.)

62 NASB-NIV Parallel New Testament in Greek and English with Interlinear: Marshall, Alfred. Regency Reference Library; Zondervan Publishing House, Grand Rapids, Michigan. USA. 1987. (Pg. 645, Heb. 10:22.)

63 NASB-NIV Parallel New Testament in Greek and English with Interlinear: Marshall, Alfred. Regency Reference Library; Zondervan Publishing House, Grand Rapids, Michigan. USA. 1987. (Pg. 641/2, Heb. 9:11-14.)

64 NASB-NIV Parallel New Testament in Greek and English with Interlinear: Marshall, Alfred. Regency Reference Library; Zondervan Publishing House, Grand Rapids, Michigan. USA. 1987. (Pg. 662, James 3:13-18.)

65 NASB-NIV Parallel New Testament in Greek and English with Interlinear: Marshall, Alfred. Regency Reference Library; Zondervan Publishing House, Grand Rapids, Michigan. USA. 1987. (Pg. 684, 1 John 1:9.)

66 The New Scofield Reference Bible, (Authorized KJV) C.I. Scofield, D.D.; Oxford University Press, New York 1967., (Pg. 1287, Col. 2:14-15.)

67 The New Scofield Reference Bible, (Authorized KJV) C.I. Scofield, D.D.; Oxford University Press, New York 1967., (Pg. 1221, Rom. 8:28-29a.)

68 NASB-NIV Parallel New Testament in Greek and English with Interlinear: Marshall, Alfred. Regency Reference Library; Zondervan Publishing House, Grand Rapids, Michigan. USA. 1987. (Pg. 576, Phil. 3:13-14.)

69 The New Scofield Reference Bible, (Authorized KJV) C.I. Scofield, D.D.; Oxford University Press, New York 1967., (Pg. 286, Josh. 24:15b.)

70 The New Scofield Reference Bible, (Authorized KJV) C.I. Scofield, D.D.; Oxford University Press, New York 1967., (Pg. 1329, James 2:19.)

71 The New Scofield Reference Bible, (Authorized KJV) C.I. Scofield, D.D.; Oxford University Press, New York 1967., (Pg. 1116, Luke 22:42.)

My Journey from Unhappiness to the Love of God

Born the youngest child of four in an argumentative family, I learned very early in life to be rebellious and constantly fight for survival. We were a church going family: however, I remember coming home from the service one day and we all were arguing. My mother turned and asked, "how can you do that, how can you go to church and come home arguing?" We all answered quickly, "It's quite easy really." Like most people of our era, going to Church, saying our prayers and grace, and following the traditions of the Church, such as Christening, and Conformation, convinced us quite clearly that we were indeed saved. Unfortunately, that was not the case, Mum was the only one who truly believed. When I was ten, my father had stopped going to Church due to a personal conflict, and so Mum asked if we could go to her denomination. He agreed to us going to both. However, the new one would not allow me to take communion, as I had not been baptised by full immersion. Following traditions again, I was then baptised at the age of 12. I enjoyed my youth group and the Church until I went nursing in NSW. The other nurses were tired of my Bible bashing ways, which we had been trained in, and decided to fix a blind date with a man named Ewan; he disliked Churches, drank heavily and smoked, all totally opposite to my life: I was 19 years of age. God alone knew he was meant to be my husband. Without attending himself, Ewan would drop me at Church and head for the pub until it was time to pick me up. Due to unforeseen circumstances he had to move to another town, so I wrote to the minister there and asked if he could find board for Ewan with a family who were Christians, but would not pressure him. Roger, the minister, purposefully determined to make friends with Ewan and as they got on so well and had many conversations, Ewan began to trust Roger. It wasn't long before he gave his heart to the LORD; and so, we entered married life as a Christian couple: or so we thought! I must say that I loved God in a fashion; I certainly believed that Jesus Christ was the Son of God, that He was born of the Virgin Mary, and eventually died in my place, was buried and then rose again on the third day. **However, there was always something missing!** Having been told constantly as a child that I was dumb and would never achieve anything in life, I lacked confidence and had a deep-seated belief in my soul that this was true. I constantly put myself down and was easily hurt. I hated life and could not understand why I had been born. I'm sure when I was younger, if I had had the courage, I would have committed suicide. I saw no point to being a woman, thinking that we were just there to be used by men. Still, deep down I thought marriage would satisfy my empty heart, and to a degree it did, but not fully. Then I thought having children would satisfy me, and certainly I loved the boys and it did help; but never did it take away the emptiness.

Ten years into our marriage, we had become too busy with our trucking business to go to Church; thankfully my mother took our sons to Sunday school, which prepared them for a later time. However, anger had entered my soul, and with Ewan away so much I continued to struggle and was constantly searching for other things to take away the emptiness.

We owed a lot of money, we had already lost our house, and now our business was failing due to truck breakdowns and firms refusing to pay on time. During this time, the government had a practice of charging all truck drivers 5c a kilometre; it was called 'road tax'. It doesn't sound much, but when one considers the severe mileage, whether we had a trailer load or not, the costs were there and with our inability to pay, they also increased. We decided to put the road tax in my name so that if I was caught, Ewan could still keep working and my Mum would happily look after our sons. It wasn't until it reached $30,000 and I was looking at a jail sentence, that we realized how foolish the decision had been. When they came for me I hid, and early the next morning we packed up and moved to an Uncle's property in the bush, still thinking we would be safe. The truck was handed back, but owing other monies as well, someone was always watching us, and the next morning they had come to repossess our Nissan E20. Later thinking about it, I felt God was saying, "You can't run away from your problems."

We had no electricity and no running water. Ewan had to build a makeshift shower under the trees and toilet to suit. I washed with the copper, grew vegetables, bought some hens and donned a long skirt and large apron. I was on the verge of a nervous breakdown and began playing the role of a pioneer lady. By the time I had made the boys' uniforms for school by hand and gotten myself organized in many other ways and routines, I was lost for something to do. Ewan had been an avid reader, but I had not. Just the same, I went to the tea chests of books, and once opening them, I discovered my Bible, a bridesmaid had given me, right on top. I picked it up numbers of times and put it down until eventually I decided, why not!

From then on for three months, I would wait until the boys left for school at 8.30am and then head into the lean-to. There I sat daily with my coffee and read my Bible until 2.30pm, when I knew my sons would soon be home. I began in Genesis as many new readers do, and by the time I got to Leviticus, I was feeling it was totally impossible for me to either please God or obey Him. For years I had a fear of death and judgement to come, but now it increased immensely.

My Dad became seriously ill, and so we went to visit with them. I decided to go to Church with Mum. A minister I disliked was preaching on Hebrews 11, and I can remember sitting there placing a circle around each time the words "by faith" were read as the minister continued through the chapter. I realized then that throughout my life I had only had a Sunday school book knowledge of the Bible, as I had never read it for myself. I did not even know that there was an explanation of what faith was in the Scriptures. I sat there listening and praying, "Well LORD, if this is the case, why was I born?" A gentle voice spoke into my soul with the reply, "You will experience many things, and learn by faith how to deal with them; and then you will help others possibly going through similar circumstances." Three times that day God showed me this to be true. I left my hometown rejoicing and decided that Hebrews was to be the next book of the Bible to read. It couldn't have been any better, as God showed me what I could not do; He had already done for me through Christ Jesus. As I read my King James Bible, the Spirit of God gave me such understanding that it was as if each letter was written especially for me. I continued from Hebrews to Revelation and then decided to go through the Gospels. It was only when I arrived at John that the love of God permeated my soul so deeply that I knew I was loved, forgiven and wanted. At last I felt needed and knew without a doubt I had been born again. *John 3:3 "Jesus answered and said to him, 'truly, truly, I say to you, unless one is born again he cannot see the kingdom of God.'"* The emptiness was gone and I knew I was complete in Him.

So, then what was the difference? As a child I believed in the Lord Jesus Christ, I knew He was the Son of God, (God come in the flesh), and that He had carried my sins on the cross, was buried and had risen again. I love John 4 where Jesus meets the woman of Samaria. He helps her to face herself and I believe that is exactly what He did for me. I had understood intellectually, and had many times been touched by His Spirit emotionally; but I had never come to the place in life where I had faced myself and saw that I was a wretched sinner. My will had been so strong that I had automatically lived in rebellion all through my life. It had to be my way or no other way, but when I recognized God's absolute holiness and saw my own wickedness, I knew I had to hand over my will to Him and allow His will to direct my life.

As an ex-truck driver, the following verse has always meant a great deal to me, simply because all our rags, covered in grease, helped me to understand how important it is to say openly to God, *"Not my will, but thine be done."* Luke 22:42

"But we are all as an unclean thing, and all our righteousnesses are as filthy rags; and we all do fade as a leaf; and our iniquities, like the wind, have taken us away." Isaiah 64:6 (KJV).

The year was 1979, and at last my life had been changed completely. What a delight to know that by the power of His Holy Spirit, God has continued to teach and correct me all the days since that momentous event.

Whatever your life has been like, and whatever it may hold in the future, I pray that you too may know His wonderful presence and love!

Printed in the United States
By Bookmasters